Presented to Purchase College
by
Gary Waller, PhD Cambridge

State University of New York
Distinguished Professor

Professor
of Literature & Cultural
Studies, and Theatre &
Performance, 1995-2019
Provost 1995-2004

Phaedra and Figaro

Robert Lowell

RACINE'S PHÈDRE

PHAEDRA

and

FIGARO

Jacques Barzun

BEAUMARCHAIS'S FIGARO'S MARRIAGE

FARRAR, STRAUS AND CUDAHY
New York

CONTENTS

Phaedra   3

Figaro's Marriage   91

DRAWINGS BY FRANK PARKER

PHAEDRA

For Miss Harriet Winslow

BACKGROUND OF THE ACTION

The story of Racine's *Phèdre* is a Greek myth. Phaedra, the wife of Theseus, the hero and king of Athens, is the daughter of Minos and Pasiphaë, the rulers of Crete. Pasiphaë coupled with a bull, and bore the Minotaur, half bull and half man, who was slain by Theseus in the maze at Crete. Phaedra falls madly in love with her stepson, Hippolytus. She is rejected by him, and falsely accuses him of trying to assault her. Theseus prays to Poseidon, the sea-god, to destroy Hippolytus; Hippolytus is destroyed. Phaedra confesses and kills herself. *Phèdre* is in some ways a miraculous translation and adaptation of Euripides' *Hippolytos*. Racine quite alters and to my mind even surpasses his wonderful original.

ON TRANSLATING PHÈDRE

Racine's plays are generally and correctly thought to be untranslatable. His syllabic alexandrines do not and cannot exist in English. We cannot reproduce his language, which is refined by the literary artifice of his contemporaries, and given a subtle realism and grandeur by the spoken idiom of Louis the Fourteenth's court. Behind each line is a for us lost knowledge of actors and actresses, the stage and the moment. Other qualities remain: the great conception, the tireless plotting, and perhaps the genius for rhetoric and versification that alone proves that the conception and plotting are honest. Matisse says somewhere that a reproduction requires as much talent for color as the original painting. I have been tormented by the fraudulence of my own heavy touch.

My meter, with important differences, is based on Dryden and Pope. In his heroic plays, Dryden uses an end-stopped couplet, loaded with inversions, heavily alliterated, and varied by short unrhymed lines. My couplet is run on, avoids inversions and alliteration, and loosens its rhythm with shifted accents and occasional extra syllables. I gain in naturalness and lose in compactness and epigrammic resonance. I have tried for an idiomatic and ageless style, but I inevitably echo the English Restoration, both in ways that are proper and in my sometimes unRacinian humor and bombast.

My version is *free,* nevertheless I have used every speech in the original, and almost every line is either translated or paraphrased. Racine is said to have written prose drafts and then versed them. We do not have the prose drafts, but I feel sure that necessities of line rhyme, etc. made for changes of phrasing and even of meaning. In versing Racine, I have taken the same liberty. Here and there, I have put in things that no French classical author would have used. Examples are the Amazon in Theramenes' first speech and the *muck* and *jelly* in Phaedra's second act speech. Such interpolations are rare, however.

No translator has had the gifts or the luck to bring Racine into our culture. It's a pity that Pope and Dryden overlooked Racine's great body of works, close to them, in favor of the inaccessible Homer and Virgil.

Racine's verse has a diamond-edge. He is perhaps the greatest poet in the French language, but he uses a smaller vocabulary than any English poet—beside him Pope and Bridges have a Shakespearean luxuriance. He has few verbally inspired lines, and in this is unlike Baudelaire and even La Fontaine. His poetry is great because of the justness of its rhythm and logic, and the glory of its hard, electric rage. I have translated as a poet, and tried to give my lines a certain dignity, speed, and flare.

ROBERT LOWELL

ACKNOWLEDGMENTS

This translation was originally written for Mr. Eric Bentley and one of his classic theater antholgies. I was helped by innumerable suggestions made by friends and experts: Elizabeth Hardwick, Eric Bentley, Jacques Barzun, Stanley Kunitz, William Alfred, Adrienne Rich, Margaret Guiton, Mary Hivnor, and I. A. Richards.

R. L.

CHARACTERS

THESEUS, *son of Aegeus and King of Athens*

PHAEDRA, *wife of Theseus and daughter of Minos and Pasiphaë*

HIPPOLYTUS, *son of Theseus and Antiope, Queen of the Amazons*

ARICIA, *princess of the royal blood of Athens*

OENONE, *nurse of Phaedra*

THERAMENES, *tutor of Hippolytus*

ISMENE, *friend of Aricia*

PANOPE, *waiting-woman of Phaedra*

Guards

Pronunciation:

Phaedra = Pheédra   Aricia = Arísha
Oenone = Eenónee   Theramenes = Therámeneés
Ismene = Ismeénee   Panope = Pánopeé
          Pasiphaë = Pásiphá-ee

ACT 1

SCENE I

Hippolytus, Theramenes

HIPPOLYTUS

No, no, my friend, we're off! Six months have passed
since Father heard the ocean howl and cast
his galley on the Aegean's skull-white froth.
Listen! The blank sea calls us—off, off, off!
I'll follow Father to the fountainhead
and marsh of hell. We're off. Alive or dead,
I'll find him.

THERAMENES

Where, my lord? I've sent a host
of veteran seamen up and down the coast;

each village, creek and cove from here to Crete
has been ransacked and questioned by my fleet;
my flagship skirted Hades' rapids, furled
sail there a day, and scoured the underworld.
Have you fresh news? New hopes? One even doubts
if noble Theseus wants his whereabouts
discovered. Does he need helpers to share
the plunder of his latest love affair;
a shipload of spectators and his son
to watch him ruin his last Amazon—
some creature, taller than a man, whose tanned
and single bosom slithers from his hand,
when he leaps to crush her like a waterfall
of honeysuckle?

HIPPOLYTUS

You are cynical,
my friend. Your insinuations wrong a king,
sick as myself of his philandering.
His heart is Phaedra's and no rivals dare
to challenge Phaedra's sole possession there.
I sail to find my father. The command
of duty calls me from this stifling land.

THERAMENES

This stifling land? Is that how you deride
this gentle province where you used to ride
the bridle-paths, pursuing happiness?
You cured your orphaned childhood's loneliness
and found a peace here you preferred to all
the blaze of Athens' brawling protocol.
A rage for exploits blinds you. Your disease
is boredom.

HIPPOLYTUS

Friend, this kingdom lost its peace,
when Father left my mother for defiled
bull-serviced Pasiphaë's child. The child
of homicidal Minos is our queen!

THERAMENES

Yes, Phaedra reigns and rules here. I have seen
you crouch before her outbursts like a cur.
When she first met you, she refused to stir
until your father drove you out of court.
The news is better now; our friends report
the queen is dying. Will you cross the seas,
desert your party and abandon Greece?
Why flee from Phaedra? Phaedra fears the night
less than she fears the day that strives to light
the universal ennui of her eye—
this dying woman, who desires to die!

HIPPOLYTUS

No, I despise her Cretan vanity,
hysteria and idle cruelty.
I fear Aricia; she alone survives
the blood-feud that destroyed her brothers' lives.

THERAMENES

Prince, Prince, forgive my laughter. Must you fly
beyond the limits of the world and die,
floating in flotsam, friendless, far from help,
and clubbed to death by Tartars in the kelp?
Why arm the shrinking violet with a knife?
Do you hate Aricia, and fear for your life,
Prince?

HIPPOLYTUS

If I hated her, I'd trust myself
and stay.

THERAMENES

Shall I explain you to yourself?
Prince, you have ceased to be that hard-mouthed, proud
and pure Hippolytus, who scorned the crowd
of common lovers once and rose above
your wayward father by despising love.
Now you justify your father, and you feel
love's poison running through you, now you kneel
and breathe the heavy incense, and a god
possesses you and revels in your blood!
Are you in love?

HIPPOLYTUS

Theramenes, when I call
and cry for help, you push me to the wall.
Why do you plague me, and try to make me fear
the qualities you taught me to revere?
I sucked in prudence with my mother's milk.
Antiope, no harlot draped in silk,
first hardened me. I was my mother's son
and not my father's. When the Amazon,
my mother, was dethroned, my mind approved
her lessons more than ever. I still loved
her bristling chastity. Later, you told
stories about my father's deeds that made me hold
back judgment—how he stood for Hercules,
a second Hercules who cleared the Cretan seas
of pirates, throttled Scirron, Cercyon,

Procrustes, Sinnis, and the giant man
of Epidaurus writhing in his gore.
He pierced the maze and killed the Minotaur.
Other things turned my stomach: that long list
of women, all refusing to resist.
Helen, caught up with all her honeyed flesh
from Sparta; Periboea, young and fresh,
already tired of Salinis. A hundred more,
their names forgotten by my father—whore
and virgin, child and mother, all deceived,
if their protestations can be believed!
Ariadne declaiming to the rocks,
her sister, Phaedra, kidnapped. Phaedra locks
the gate at last! You know how often I
would weary, fall to nodding and deny
the possibility of hearing the whole
ignoble, dull, insipid boast unroll.
And now I too must fall. The gods have made me creep.
How can I be in love? I have no specious heap
of honors, friend. No mastered monsters drape
my shoulders—Theseus' excuse to rape
at will. Suppose I chose a woman. Why
choose an orphan? Aricia is eternally
cut off from marriage, lest she breed
successors to her fierce brothers, and seed
the land with treason. Father only grants
her life on one condition. This—he wants
no bridal torch to burn for her. Unwooed
and childless, she must answer for the blood
her brothers shed. How can I marry her,
gaily subvert our kingdom's character,
and sail on the high seas of love?

THERAMENES

You'll prove
nothing by reason, for you are in love.
Theseus' injustice to Aricia throws
her in the light; your eyes he wished to close
are open. She dazzles you. Her pitiful
seclusion makes her doubly terrible.
Does this innocent passion freeze your blood?
There's sweetness in it. Is your only good
the dismal famine of your chastity?
You shun your father's path? Where would you be,
Prince, if Antiope had never burned
chastely for Theseus? Love, my lord, has turned
the head of Hercules, and thousands—fired
the forge of Vulcan! All your uninspired,
cold moralizing is nothing, Prince. You have changed!
Now no one sees you riding, half-deranged
along the sand-bars, where you drove your horse
and foaming chariot with all your force,
tilting and staggering upright through the surf—
far from their usual course across the turf.
The woods are quiet . . . How your eyes hang down!
You often murmur and forget to frown.
All's out, Prince. You're in love; you burn. Flames, flames,
Prince! A dissimulated sickness maims
the youthful quickness of your daring. Does
lovely Aricia haunt you?

HIPPOLYTUS

Friend, spare us.
I sail to find my father.

THERAMENES

Will you see
Phaedra before you go?

HIPPOLYTUS

I mean to be
here when she comes. Go, tell her. I will do
my duty. Wait, I see her nurse. What new
troubles torment her?

SCENE II

Hippolytus, Theramenes, Oenone

OENONE

Who has griefs like mine,
my lord? I cannot help the queen in her decline.
Although I sit beside her day and night,
she shuts her eyes and withers in my sight.
An eternal tumult roisters through her head,
panics her sleep, and drags her from her bed.
Just now she fled me at the prime
of day to see the sun for the last time.
She's coming.

HIPPOLYTUS

So! I'll steal away. My flight
removes a hateful object from her sight.

SCENE III

Phaedra, Oenone

PHAEDRA

Dearest, we'll go no further. I must rest.
I'll sit here. My emotions shake my breast,
the sunlight throws black bars across my eyes.
My knees give. If I fall, why should I rise,
Nurse?

OENONE

Heaven help us! Let me comfort you.

PHAEDRA

Tear off these gross, official rings, undo
these royal veils. They drag me to the ground.
Why have you frilled me, laced me, crowned me, and wound
my hair in turrets? All your skill torments
and chokes me. I am crushed by ornaments.
Everything hurts me, and drags me to my knees!

OENONE

Now this, now that, Madam. You never cease
commanding us, then cancelling your commands.
You feel your strength return, summon all hands
to dress you like a bride, then say you choke!
We open all the windows, fetch a cloak,
rush you outdoors. It's no use, you decide
that sunlight kills you, and only want to hide.

PHAEDRA

I feel the heavens' royal radiance cool
and fail, as if it feared my terrible
shame has destroyed its right to shine on men.
I'll never look upon the sun again.

OENONE

Renunciation or renunciation!
Now you slander the source of your creation.
Why do you run to death and tear your hair?

PHAEDRA

Oh God, take me to some sunless forest lair . . .
There hoof-beats raise a dust-cloud, and my eye
follows a horseman outlined on the sky!

OENONE

What's this, my lady?

PHAEDRA

I have lost my mind.
Where am I? Oh forget my words! I find
I've lost the habit now of talking sense.
My face is red and guilty—evidence
of treason! I've betrayed my darkest fears,
Nurse, and my eyes, despite me, fill with tears.

OENONE

Lady, if you must weep, weep for your silence
that filled your days and mine with violence.
Ah deaf to argument and numb to care,
you have no mercy. Spare me, spare
yourself. Your blood is like polluted water,

fouling a mind desiring its own slaughter.
The sun has died and shadows filled the skies
thrice now, since you have closed your eyes;
the day has broken through the night's content
thrice now, since you have tasted nourishment.
Is your salvation from your terrified
conscience this passive, servile suicide?
Lady, your madness harms the gods who gave
you life, betrays your husband. Who will save
your children? Your downfall will orphan them,
deprive them of their kingdom, and condemn
their lives and future to the discipline
of one who abhors you and all your kin,
a tyrant suckled by an amazon,
Hippolytus . . .

PHAEDRA

Oh God!

OENONE

You still hate someone;
thank heaven for that, Madam!

PHAEDRA

You spoke his name!

OENONE

Hippolytus, Hippolytus! There's hope
in hatred, Lady. Give your anger rope.
I love your anger. If the winds of love
and fury stir you, you will live. Above
your children towers this foreigner, this child
of Scythian cannibals, now wild

to ruin the kingdom, master Greece, and choke
the children of the gods beneath his yoke.
Why dawdle? Why deliberate at length?
Oh, gather up your dissipated strength.

PHAEDRA

I've lived too long.

OENONE

Always, always agonized!
Is your conscience still stunned and paralyzed?
Do you think you have washed your hands in blood?

PHAEDRA

Thank God, my hands are clean still. Would to God
my heart were innocent!

OENONE

Your heart, your heart!
What have you done that tears your soul apart?

PHAEDRA

I've said too much. Oenone, let me die;
by dying I shall escape blasphemy.

OENONE

Search for another hand to close your eyes.
Oh cruel Queen, I see that you despise
my sorrow and devotion. I'll die first,
and end the anguish of this service cursed
by your perversity. A thousand roads
always lie open to the killing gods.
I'll choose the nearest. Lady, tell me how

Oenone's love has failed you. Will you allow
your nurse to die, your nurse, who gave up all—
nation, parents, children, to serve in thrall.
I saved you from your mother, King Minos' wife!
Will your death pay me for giving up my life?

PHAEDRA

What I could tell you, I have told you. Nurse,
only my silence saves me from the curse
of heaven.

OENONE

How could you tell me anything
worse than watching you dying?

PHAEDRA

I would bring
my life and rank dishonor. What can I say
to save myself, or put off death a day.

OENONE

Ah Lady, I implore you by my tears,
and by your suffering body. Heaven hears,
and knows the truth already. Let me see.

PHAEDRA

Stand up.

OENONE

Your hesitation's killing me!

PHAEDRA

What can I tell you? How the gods reprove
me!

OENONE

Speak!

PHAEDRA

Oh Venus, murdering Venus! love
gored Pasiphaë with the bull.

OENONE

Forget
your mother! When she died, she paid her debt.

PHAEDRA

Oh Ariadne, oh my Sister, lost
for love of Theseus on that rocky coast.

OENONE

Lady, what nervous languor makes you rave
against your family; they are in the grave.

PHAEDRA

Remorseless Aphrodite drives me. I,
my race's last and worst love-victim, die.

OENONE

Are you in love?

PHAEDRA

I am insane with love!

OENONE

Who
is he?

PHAEDRA

I'll tell you. Nothing love can do
could equal . . . Nurse, I am in love. The shame
kills me. I love the . . . Do not ask his name.

OENONE

Who?

PHAEDRA

Nurse, you know my old loathing for the son
of Theseus and the barbarous amazon?

OENONE

Hippolytus! My God, oh my God!

PHAEDRA

You,
not I, have named him.

OENONE

What can you do,
but die? Your words have turned my blood to ice.
Oh righteous heavens, must the blasphemies
of Pasiphaë fall upon her daughter?
Her Furies strike us down across the water.
Why did we come here?

PHAEDRA

My evil comes from farther off. In May,
in brilliant Athens, on my marriage day,
I turned aside for shelter from the smile
of Theseus. Death was frowning in an aisle—
Hippolytus! I saw his face, turned white!

My lost and dazzled eyes saw only night,
capricious burnings flickered through my bleak
abandoned flesh. I could not breathe or speak.
I faced my flaming executioner,
Aphrodite, my mother's murderer!
I tried to calm her wrath by flowers and praise,
I built her a temple, fretted months and days
on decoration. I even hoped to find
symbols and stays for my distracted mind,
searching the guts of sacrificial steers.
Yet when my erring passions, mutineers
to virtue, offered incense at the shrine
of love, I failed to silence the malign
Goddess. Alas, my hungry open mouth,
thirsting with adoration, tasted drouth—
Venus resigned her altar to my new lord—
and even while I was praying, I adored
Hippolytus above the sacred flame,
now offered to his name I could not name.
I fled him, yet he stormed me in disguise,
and seemed to watch me from his father's eyes.
I even turned against myself, screwed up
my slack courage to fury, and would not stop
shrieking and raging, till half-dead with love
and the hatred of a stepmother, I drove
Hippolytus in exile from the rest
and strenuous wardship of his father's breast.
Then I could breathe, Oenone; he was gone;
my lazy, nerveless days meandered on
through dreams and daydreams, like a stately carriage
touring the level landscape of my marriage.
Yet nothing worked. My husband sent me here
to Troezen, far from Athens; once again the dear

face shattered me; I saw Hippolytus
each day, and felt my ancient, venomous
passion tear my body limb from limb;
naked Venus was clawing down her victim.
What could I do? Each moment, terrified
by loose diseased emotions, now I cried
for death to save my glory and expel
my gloomy frenzy from this world, my hell.
And yet your tears and words bewildered me,
and so endangered my tranquillity,
at last I spoke. Nurse, I shall not repent,
if you will leave me the passive content
of dry silence and solitude.

SCENE IV

Phaedra, Oenone, Panope

PANOPE

My heart breaks. Would to God, I could refuse
to tell your majesty my evil news.
The King is dead! Listen, the heavens ring
with shouts and lamentations for the King.

PHAEDRA

The King is dead? What's this?

PANOPE

              In vain
you beg the gods to send him back again.

Hippolytus has heard the true report,
he is already heading for the port.

PHAEDRA

Oh God!

PANOPE

They've heard in Athens. Everyone
is joining factions—some salute your son,
others are calling for Hippolytus;
they want him to reform and harden us—
even Aricia claims the loyalty
of a fanatical minority.
The Prince's captains have recalled their men.
His flag is up and now he sails again
for Athens. Queen, if he appear there now,
he'll drag the people with him!

OENONE

Stop, allow
the Queen a little respite for her grief.
She hears you, and will act for our relief.

SCENE V

Phaedra, Oenone

OENONE

I'd given up persuading you to live;
death was your refuge, only death could give

you peace and save your troubled glory. I
myself desired to follow you, and die.
But this catastrophe prescribes new laws:
the king is dead, and for the king who was,
fate offers you his kingdom. You have a son;
he should be king! If you abandon
him, he'll be a slave. The gods, his ancestors,
will curse and drive you on your fatal course.
Live! Who'll condemn you if you love and woo
the Prince? Your stepson is no kin to you,
now that your royal husband's death has cut
and freed you from the throttling marriage-knot.
Do not torment the Prince with persecution,
and give a leader to the revolution;
no, win his friendship, bind him to your side.
Give him this city and its countryside.
He will renounce the walls of Athens, piled
stone on stone by Minerva for your child.
Stand with Hippolytus, annihilate
Aricia's faction, and possess the state!

PHAEDRA

So be it! Your superior force has won.
I will live if compassion for my son,
devotion to the Prince, and love of power
can give me courage in this fearful hour.

ACT 2

SCENE I

Aricia, Ismene

ARICIA

What's this? The Prince has sent a messenger?
The Prince begs me to wait and meet him here?
The Prince begs! Goose, you've lost your feeble wits!

ISMENE

Lady, be calm. These are the benefits
of Theseus' death: first Prince Hippolytus
comes courting favors; soon the populous
cities of Greece will follow—they will eat
out of your hand, Princess, and kiss your feet.

ARICIA

This felon's hand, this slave's! My dear, your news
is only frivolous gossip, I refuse
to hope.

ISMENE

Ah Princess, the just powers of hell
have struck. Theseus has joined your brothers!

ARICIA

Tell

me how he died.

ISMENE

Princess, fearful tales
are circulating. Sailors saw his sails,
his infamous black sails, spin round and round
in Charybdis' whirlpool; all hands were drowned.
Yet others say on better evidence
that Theseus and Pirithoüs passed the dense
darkness of hell to rape Persephone.
Pirithoüs was murdered by the hound;
Theseus, still living, was buried in the ground.

ARICIA

This is an old wives' tale. Only the dead
enter the underworld, and see the bed
of Queen Persephone. What brought him there?

ISMENE

Princess, the King is dead—dead! Everywhere
men know and mourn. Already our worshipping
townsmen acclaim Hippolytus for their king;

in her great palace, Phaedra, the self-styled
regent, rages and trembles for her child.

ARICIA

What makes you think the puritanical
son of Theseus is human. Will he recall
my sentence and relent?

ISMENE

I know he will.

ARICIA

You know nothing about him. He would kill
a woman, rather than be kind to one.
That wolf-cub of a fighting amazon
hates me above all women. He would walk
from here to hell, rather than hear me talk.

ISMENE

Do you know Hippolytus? Listen to me.
His famous, blasphemous frigidity,
what is it, when you've seen him close at hand?
I've watched him like a hawk, and seen him stand
shaking beside you—all his reputation
for hating womenkind bears no relation
to what I saw. He couldn't take his eyes
off you! His eyes speak what his tongue denies.

ARICIA

I can't believe you. Your story's absurd!
How greedily I listen to each word!
Ismene, you know me, you know how my heart
was reared on death, and always set apart

from what it cherished—can this plaything of
the gods and furies feel the peace of love?
What sights I've seen, Ismene! "Heads will roll,"
my brothers told me, "we will rule." I, the sole
survivor of those fabulous kings, who tilled
the soil of Greece, have seen my brothers killed,
six brothers murdered! In a single hour,
the tyrant, Theseus, lopped them in their flower.
The monster spared my life, and yet decreed
the torments of this childless life I lead
in exile, where no Greek can look on me;
my forced, perpetual virginity
preserves his crown; no son shall bear my name
or blow my brothers' ashes into flame.
Ismene, you know how well his tyranny
favors my temperament and strengthens me
to guard the honor of my reputation;
his rigor fortified my inclination.
How could I test his son's civilities?
I'd never even seen him with my eyes!
I'd never seen him. I'd restrained my eye,
that giddy nerve, from dwelling thoughtlessly
upon his outward grace and beauty—on mere
embellishments of nature, a veneer
the Prince himself despises and ignores.
My heart loves nobler virtues, and adores
in him his father's hard intelligence.
He has his father's daring and a sense
of honor his father lacks. Let me confess,
I love him for his lofty haughtiness
never submitted to a woman's yoke.
How could Phaedra's splendid marriage provoke
my jealousy? Have I so little pride,

I'd snatch at a rake's heart, a heart denied
to none—all riddled, opened up to let
thousands pass in like water through a net?
To carry sorrows to a heart, alone
untouched by passion, inflexible as stone,
to fasten my dominion on a force
as nervous as a never-harnessed horse—
this stirs me, this enflames me. Devilish Zeus
is easier mastered than Hippolytus;
heaven's love-infatuated emperor
confers less glory on his conqueror!
Ismene, I'm afraid. Why should I boast?
His very virtues I admire most
threaten to rise and throw me from the brink
of hope. What girlish folly made me think
Hippolytus could love Aricia?

ISMENE

Here
he is. He loves you, Princess. Have no fear.

SCENE II

Aricia, Ismene, Hippolytus

HIPPOLYTUS

Princess, before
I leave here, I must tell you what's in store
for you in Greece. Alas, my father's dead.
The fierce forebodings that disquieted

my peace are true. Death, only death, could hide
his valor from this world he pacified.
The homicidal Fates will not release
the comrade, friend and peer of Hercules.
Princess, I trust your hate will not resent
honors whose justice is self-evident.
A single hope alleviates my grief,
Princess, I hope to offer you relief.
I now revoke a law whose cruelty
has pained my conscience. Princess, you are free
to marry. Oh enjoy this province, whose
honest, unhesitating subjects choose
Hippolytus for king. Live free as air,
here, free as I am, much more free!

ARICIA

                              I dare
not hope. You are too gracious. Can you free
Aricia from your father's stern decree?

HIPPOLYTUS

Princess, the Athenian people, torn in two
between myself and Phaedra's son, want you.

ARICIA

Want me, my Lord!

HIPPOLYTUS

                    I've no illusions. Lame
Athenian precedents condemn my claim,
because my mother was a foreigner.
But what is that? If my only rival were
my younger brother, his minority

would clear my legal disability.
However, a better claim than his or mine
now favors you, ennobled by the line
of great Erectheus. Your direct descent
sets you before my father; he was only lent
this kingdom by adoption. Once the common
Athenian, dazed by Theseus' superhuman
energies, had no longing to exhume
the rights that rushed your brothers to their doom.
Now Athens calls you home; the ancient feud
too long has stained the sacred olive wood;
blood festers in the furrows of our soil
to blight its fruits and scorch the farmer's toil.
This province suits me; let the vines of Crete
offer my brother a secure retreat.
The rest is yours. All Attica is yours;
I go to win you what your right assures.

ARICIA

Am I awake, my lord? Your sayings seem
like weird phantasmagoria in a dream.
How can your sparkling promises be true?
Some god, my lord, some god, has entered you!
How justly you are worshiped in this town;
oh how the truth surpasses your renown!
You wish to endow me with your heritage!
I only hoped you would not hate me. This rage
your father felt, how can you put it by
and treat me kindly?

HIPPOLYTUS

Princess, is my eye
blind to beauty? Am I a bear, a bull, a boar,

some abortion fathered by the Minotaur?
Some one-eyed Cyclops, able to resist
Aricia's loveliness and still exist?
How can a man stand up against your grace?

ARICIA

My lord, my lord!

HIPPOLYTUS

     I cannot hide my face,
Princess! I'm driven. Why does my violence
so silence reason and intelligence?
Must I be still, and let my adoration
simmer away in silent resignation?
Princess, I've lost all power to restrain
myself. You see a madman, whose insane
pride hated love, and hoped to sit ashore,
watching the galleys founder in the war;
I was Diana's liegeman, dressed in steel.
I hoped to trample love beneath my heel—
alas, the flaming Venus burns me down,
I am the last dependent on her crown.
What left me charred and writhing in her clutch?
A single moment and a single touch.
Six months now, bounding like a wounded stag,
I've tried to shake this poisoned dart, and drag
myself to safety from your eyes that blind
when present, and when absent leave behind
volleys of burning arrows in my mind.
Ah Princess, shall I dive into the sea,
or steal the wings of Icarus to flee
love's Midas' touch that turns my world to gold?
Your image drives me stumbling through the cold,

floods my deserted forest caves with light,
darkens the day and dazzles through my night.
I'm grafted to your side by all I see;
all things unite us and imprison me.
I have no courage for the Spartan exercise
that trained my hand and steeled my energies.
Where are my horses? I forget their names.
My triumphs with my chariot at the games
no longer give me strength to mount a horse.
The ocean drives me shuddering from its shores.
Does such a savage conquest make you blush?
My boorish gestures, headlong cries that rush
at you like formless monsters from the sea?
Ah, Princess, hear me! Your serenity
must pardon the distortions of a weak
and new-born lover, forced by you to speak
love's foreign language, words that snarl and yelp . . .
I never could have spoken without your help.

SCENE III

Aricia, Ismene, Hippolytus, Theramenes

THERAMENES

I announce the Queen. She comes hurriedly,
looking for you.

HIPPOLYTUS

For me!

THERAMENES

          Don't ask me why;
she insisted. I promised I'd prevail
on you to speak with her before you sail.

HIPPOLYTUS

What can she want to hear? What can I say?

ARICIA

Wait for her, here! You cannot turn away.
Forget her malice. Hating her will serve
no purpose. Wait for her! Her tears deserve
your pity.

HIPPOLYTUS

        You're going, Princess? And I must go
to Athens, far from you. How shall I know
if you accept my love.

ARICIA

          My lord, pursue
your gracious promise. Do what you must do,
make Athens tributary to my rule.
Nothing you offer is unacceptable;
yet this empire, so great, so glorious,
is the least precious of your gifts to us.

SCENE IV

Hippolytus, Theramenes

HIPPOLYTUS

We're ready. Wait, the Queen's here. I need you.
You must interrupt this tedious interview.
Hurry down to the ship, then rush back, pale
and breathless. Say the wind's up and we must sail.

SCENE V

Hippolytus, Oenone, Phaedra

PHAEDRA

He's here! Why does he scowl and look away
from me? What shall I do? What shall I say?

OENONE

Speak for your son, he has no other patron.

PHAEDRA

Why are you so impatient to be gone
from us, my lord? Stay! we will weep together.
Pity my son; he too has lost his father.
My own death's near. Rebellion, sick with wrongs,
now like a sea-beast, lifts its slimey prongs,
its muck, its jelly. You alone now stand

to save the state. Who else can understand
a mother? I forget. You will not hear
me! An enemy deserves no pity. I fear
your anger. Must my son, your brother, Prince,
be punished for his cruel mother's sins?

HIPPOLYTUS

I've no such thoughts.

PHAEDRA

         I persecuted you
blindly, and now you have good reason to
return my impudence. How could you find
the motivation of this heart and mind
that scourged and tortured you, till you began
to lose the calm composure of a man,
and dwindle to a harsh and sullen boy,
a thing of ice, unable to enjoy
the charms of any civilized resource
except the heavy friendship of your horse,
that whirled you far from women, court and throne,
to course the savage woods for wolves alone?
You have good reason, yet if pain's a measure,
no one has less deserved your stern displeasure.
My lord, no one has more deserved compassion.

HIPPOLYTUS

Lady, I understand a mother's passion,
a mother jealous for her children's rights.
How can she spare a first wife's son? Long nights
of plotting, devious ways of quarrelling—
a madhouse! What else can remarriage bring?

Another would have shown equal hostility,
pushed her advantage more outrageously.

PHAEDRA

My lord, if you had known how far my love
and yearning have exalted me above
this usual weakness . . . Our afflicting kinship
is ending . . .

HIPPOLYTUS

          Madam, the precious minutes slip
by, I fatigue you. Fight against your fears.
Perhaps Poseidon has listened to our tears,
perhaps your husband's still alive. He hears
us, he is surging home—only a short
day's cruise conceals him, as he scuds for port.

PHAEDRA

That's folly, my lord. Who has twice visited
black Hades and the river of the dead
and returned? No, the poisonous Acheron
never lets go. Theseus drifts on and on,
a gutted galley on that clotted waste—
he woos, he wins Persephone, the chaste . . .
What am I saying? Theseus is not dead.
He lives in you. He speaks, he's taller by a head,
I see him, touch him, and my heart—a reef . . .
Ah Prince, I wander. Love betrays my grief . . .

HIPPOLYTUS

No, no, my father lives. Lady, the blind

furies release him; in your loyal mind,
love's fullness holds him, and he cannot die.

PHAEDRA

I hunger for Theseus. Always in my eye
he wanders, not as he appeared in hell,
lascivious eulogist of any belle
he found there, from the lowest to the Queen;
no, faithful, airy, just a little mean
through virtue, charming all, yet young and new,
as we would paint a god—as I now see you!
Your valiant shyness would have graced his speech,
he would have had your stature, eyes, and reach,
Prince, when he flashed across our Cretan waters,
the loved enslaver of King Minos' daughters.
Where were you? How could he conscript the flower
of Athens' youth against my father's power,
and ignore you? You were too young, they say;
you should have voyaged as a stowaway.
No dawdling bypath would have saved our bull,
when your just vengeance thundered through its skull.
There, light of foot, and certain of your goal,
you would have struck my brother's monstrous soul,
and pierced our maze's slow meanders, led
by Ariadne and her subtle thread.
By Ariadne? Prince, I would have fought
for precedence; my every flaming thought,
love-quickened, would have shot you through the dark,
straight as an arrow to your quaking mark.
Could I have waited, panting, perishing,
entrusting your survival to a string,
like Ariadne, when she skulked behind,
there at the portal, to bemuse her mind

among the solemn cloisters of the porch?
No, Phaedra would have snatched your burning torch,
and lunged before you, reeling like a priest
of Dionysus to distract the beast.
I would have reached the final corridor
a lap before you, and killed the Minotaur!
Lost in the labyrinth, and at your side,
would it have mattered, if I lived or died?

HIPPOLYTUS

What are you saying, Madam? You forget
my father is your husband!

PHAEDRA

I have let
you see my grief for Theseus! How could I
forget my honor and my majesty,
Prince?

HIPPOLYTUS

Madam, forgive me! My foolish youth
conjectured hideous untruths from your truth.
I cannot face my insolence. Farewell . . .

PHAEDRA

You monster! You understood me too well!
Why do you hang there, speechless, petrified,
polite! My mind whirls. What have I to hide?
Phaedra in all her madness stands before you.
I love you! Fool, I love you, I adore you!
Do not imagine that my mind approved
my first defection, Prince, or that I loved
your youth light-heartedly, and fed my treason

with cowardly compliance, till I lost my reason.
I wished to hate you, but the gods corrupt
us; though I never suffered their abrupt
seductions, shattering advances, I
too bear their sensual lightnings in my thigh.
I too am dying. I have felt the heat
that drove my mother through the fields of Crete,
the bride of Minos, dying for the full
magnetic April thunders of the bull.
I struggled with my sickness, but I found
no grace or magic to preserve my sound
intelligence and honor from this lust,
plowing my body with its horny thrust.
At first I fled you, and when this fell short
of safety, Prince, I exiled you from court.
Alas, my violence to resist you made
my face inhuman, hateful. I was afraid
to kiss my husband lest I love his son.
I made you fear me (this was easily done);
you loathed me more, I ached for you no less.
Misfortune magnified your loveliness.
I grew so wrung and wasted, men mistook
me for the Sibyl. If you could bear to look
your eyes would tell you. Do you believe my passion
is voluntary? That my obscene confession
is some dark trick, some oily artifice?
I came to beg you not to sacrifice
my son, already uncertain of his life.
Ridiculous, mad embassy, for a wife
who loves her stepson! Prince, I only spoke
about myself! Avenge yourself, invoke
your father; a worse monster threatens you
than any Theseus ever fought and slew.

The wife of Theseus loves Hippolytus!
See, Prince! Look, this monster, ravenous
for her execution, will not flinch.
I want your sword's spasmodic final inch.

OENONE

Madam, put down this weapon. Your distress
attracts the people. Fly these witnesses.
Hurry! Stop kneeling! What a time to pray!

SCENE VI

Theramenes, Hippolytus

THERAMENES

Is this Phaedra, fleeing, or rather dragged away
sobbing? Where is your sword? Who tore
this empty scabbard from your belt?

HIPPOLYTUS

                                No more!
Oh let me get away! I face disaster.
Horrors unnerve me. Help! I cannot master
my terror. Phaedra . . . No, I won't expose
her. No! Something I do not dare disclose . . .

THERAMENES

Our ship is ready, but before you leave,
listen! Prince, what we never would believe
has happened: Athens has voted for your brother.

The citizens have made him king. His mother
is regent.

HIPPOLYTUS

Phaedra is in power!

THERAMENES

An envoy sent from Athens came this hour
to place the scepter in her hands. Her son
is king.

HIPPOLYTUS

Almighty gods, you know this woman!
Is it her spotless virtue you reward?

THERAMENES

I've heard a rumor. Someone swam aboard
a ship off Epirus. He claims the King
is still alive. I've searched. I know the thing
is nonsense.

HIPPOLYTUS

Search! Nothing must be neglected.
If the king's dead, I'll rouse the disaffected
people, crown Aricia, and place our lands,
our people, and our lives in worthy hands.

ACT 3

SCENE I

Phaedra, Oenone

PHAEDRA

Why do my people rush to crown me queen?
Who can even want to see me? They have seen
my downfall. Will their praise deliver me?
Oh bury me at the bottom of the sea!
Nurse, I have said too much! Led on by you,
I've said what no one should have listened to.
He listened. How could he pretend my drift
was hidden? Something held him, and made him shift
his ground . . . He only wanted to depart
and hide, while I was pouring out my heart.
Oh how his blushing multiplied my shame!

Why did you hold me back! You are to blame,
Oenone. But for you, I would have killed
myself. Would he have stood there, iron-willed
and merciless, while I fell upon his sword?
He would have snatched it, held me, and restored
my life. No! No!

OENONE

Control yourself! No peace
comes from surrendering to your disease,
Madam. Oh daughter of the kings of Crete,
why are you weeping and fawning at the feet
of this barbarian, less afraid of fate
than of a woman? You must rule the state.

PHAEDRA

Can I, who have no courage to restrain
the insurrection of my passions, reign?
Will the Athenians trust their sovereignty
to me? Love's despotism is crushing me,
I am ruined.

OENONE

Fly!

PHAEDRA

How can I leave him?

OENONE

Lady, you have already banished him.
Can't you take flight?

PHAEDRA

The time for flight has passed.
He knows me now. I rushed beyond the last

limits of modesty, when I confessed.
Hope was no longer blasting through my breast;
I was resigned to hopelessness and death,
and gasping out my last innocent breath,
Oenone, when you forced me back to life.
You thought I was no longer Theseus' wife,
and let me feel that I was free to love.

OENONE

I would have done anything to remove
your danger. Whether I'm guilty or innocent
is all the same to me. Your punishment
should fall on one who tried to kill you, not
on poor Oenone. Lady, you must plot
and sacrifice this monster, whose unjust
abhorrence left you dying in the dust.
Oh humble him, undo him, oh despise
him! Lady, you must see him with my eyes.

PHAEDRA

Oenone, he was nourished in the woods;
he is all shyness and ungracious moods
because the forests left him half-inhuman.
He's never heard love spoken by a woman!
We've gone too far. Oenone, we're unwise;
perhaps the young man's silence was surprise.

OENONE

His mother, the amazon, was never moved
by men.

PHAEDRA

The boy exists. She must have loved!

OENONE

He has a sullen hatred for our sex.

PHAEDRA

Oh, all the better; rivals will not vex
my chances. Your advice is out of season;
now you must serve my frenzy, not my reason!
You tell me love has never touched his heart;
we'll look, we'll find an undefended part.
He's turned his bronze prows seaward; look, the wind
already blows like a trumpeter behind
his bulging canvas! The Acropolis
of Athens and its empire shall be his!
Hurry, Oenone, hunt the young man down,
blind him with dazzling visions of the crown.
Go tell him I relinquish my command,
I only want the guidance of his hand.
Let him assume these powers that weary me,
he will instruct my son in sovereignty.
Perhaps he will adopt my son, and be
the son and mother's one divinity!
Oenone, rush to him, use every means
to bend and win him; if he fears the Queen's
too proud, he'll listen to her slave. Plead, groan,
insist, say I am giving him my throne . . .
No, say I'm dying!

SCENE II

Phaedra

PHAEDRA

       Implacable Aphrodite, now you see
the depths to which your tireless cruelty
has driven Phaedra—here is my bosom;
every thrust and arrow his struck home!
Oh Goddess, if you hunger for renown,
rise now, and shoot a worthier victim down!
Conquer the barbarous Hippolytus,
who mocks the graces and the power of Venus,
and gazes on your godhead with disgust.
Avenge me, Venus! See, my cause is just,
my cause is yours. Oh bend him to my will! . . .
You're back, Oenone? Does he hate me still?

SCENE III

Phaedra, Oenone

OENONE

Your love is folly, dash it from your soul,
gather your scattered pride and self-control,
Madam! I've seen the royal ship arrive.
Theseus is back, Theseus is still alive!
Thousands of voices thunder from the docks.

People are waving flags and climbing rocks.
While I was looking for Hippolytus . . .

PHAEDRA

My husband's living! Must you trouble us
by talking? What am I living for?
He lives, Oenone, let me hear no more
about it.

OENONE

Why?

PHAEDRA

I told you, but my fears
were stilled, alas, and smothered by your tears.
Had I died this morning, I might have faced
the gods. I heeded you and die disgraced!

OENONE

You are disgraced!

PHAEDRA

Oh Gods of wrath,
how far I've travelled on my dangerous path!
I go to meet my husband; at his side
will stand Hippolytus. How shall I hide
my thick adulterous passion for this youth,
who has rejected me, and knows the truth?
Will the stern Prince stand smiling and approve
the labored histrionics of my love
for Theseus, see my lips, still languishing
for his, betray his father and his King?
Will he not draw his sword and strike me dead?

Suppose he spares me? What if nothing's said?
Am I a gorgon, or Circe, or the infidel
Medea, stifled by the flames of hell,
yet rising like Aphrodite from the sea,
refreshed and radiant with indecency?
Can I kiss Theseus with dissembled poise?
I think each stone and pillar has a voice.
The very dust rises to disabuse
my husband—to defame me and accuse!
Oenone, I want to die. Death will give
me freedom; oh it's nothing not to live;
death to the unhappy's no catastrophe!
I fear the name that must live after me,
and crush my son until the end of time.
Is his inheritance his mother's crime,
his right to curse me, when my pollution stains
the blood of heaven bubbling in his veins?
The day will come, alas, the day will come,
when nothing will be left to save him from
the voices of despair. If he should live
he'll flee his subjects like a fugitive.

OENONE

He has my pity. Who has ever built
firmer foundations to expose her guilt?
But why expose your son? Is your contribution
for his defense to serve the prosecution?
Suppose you kill yourself? The world will say
you fled your outraged husband in dismay.
Could there be stronger evidence and proof
than Phaedra crushed beneath the horse's hoof
of blasphemous self-destruction to convince
the crowds who'll dance attendance on the Prince?

The crowds will mob your children when they hear
their defamation by a foreigner!
Wouldn't you rather see earth bury us?
Tell me, do you still love Hippolytus?

PHAEDRA

I see him as a beast, who'd murder us.

OENONE

Madam, let the positions be reversed!
You fear the Prince; you must accuse him first.
Who'll dare assert your story is untrue,
if all the evidence shall speak for you:
your present grief, your past despair of mind,
the Prince's sword so luckily left behind?
Do you think Theseus will oppose his son's
second exile? He has consented once!

PHAEDRA

How dare I take this murderous, plunging course?

OENONE

I tremble, Lady, I too feel remorse.
If death could rescue you from infamy,
Madam, I too would follow you and die.
Help me by being silent. I will speak
in such a way the King will only seek
a bloodless exile to assert his rights.
A father is still a father when he smites,
You shudder at this evil sacrifice,
but nothing's evil or too high a price
to save your menaced honor from defeat.
Ah Minos, Minos, you defended Crete

by killing young men? Help us! If the cost
for saving Phaedra is a holocaust
of virtue, Minos, you must sanctify
our undertaking, or watch your daughter die.
I see the King.

PHAEDRA

I see Hippolytus!

SCENE IV

Phaedra, Theseus, Hippolytus, Oenone

THESEUS

Fate's heard me, Phaedra, and removed the bar
that kept me from your arms.

PHAEDRA

                    Theseus, stop where you are!
Your raptures and endearments are profane.
Your arm must never comfort me again.
You have been wronged, the gods who spared your life
have used your absence to disgrace your wife,
unworthy now to please you or come near.
My only refuge is to disappear.

SCENE V

Theseus, Hippolytus

THESEUS

What a strange welcome! This bewilders me.
My son, what's happened?

HIPPOLYTUS

                    Phaedra holds the key.
Ask Phaedra. If you love me, let me leave
this kingdom. I'm determined to achieve
some action that will show my strength. I fear
Phaedra. I am afraid of living here,

THESEUS

My son, you want to leave me?

HIPPOLYTUS

                    I never sought
her grace or favor. Your decision brought
her here from Athens. Your desires prevailed
against my judgment, Father, when you sailed
leaving Phaedra and Aricia in my care.
I've done my duty, now I must prepare
for sterner actions, I must test my skill
on monsters far more dangerous to kill
than any wolf or eagle in this wood.
Release me, I too must prove my manhood.
Oh Father, you were hardly half my age,
when herds of giants writhed before your rage—

you were already famous as the scourge
of insolence. Our people saw you purge
the pirates from the shores of Greece and Thrace,
the harmless merchantman was free to race
the winds, and weary Hercules could pause
from slaughter, knowing you upheld his cause.
The world revered you. I am still unknown;
even my mother's deeds surpass my own.
Some tyrants have escaped you; let me meet
with them and throw their bodies at your feet.
I'll drag them from their wolf-holes; if I die,
my death will show I struggled worthily.
Oh, Father, raise me from oblivion;
my deeds shall tell the universe I am your son.

THESEUS

What do I see? Oh gods, what horror drives
my queen and children fleeing for their lives
before me? If so little warmth remains,
oh why did you release me from my chains?
Why am I hated, and so little loved?
I had a friend, just one. His folly moved
me till I aided his conspiracy
to ravish Queen Persephone.
The gods, tormented by our blasphemous
designs, befogged our minds and blinded us—
we invaded Epirus instead of hell.
There a diseased and subtle tyrant fell
upon us as we slept, and while I stood
by, helpless, monsters crazed for human blood
consumed Pirithoüs. I myself was chained
fast in a death-deep dungeon. I remained
six months there, then the gods had pity,

and put me in possession of the city.
I killed the tyrant; now his body feasts
the famished, pampered bellies of his beasts.
At last, I voyaged home, cast anchor, furled
my sails. When I was rushing to my world—
what am I saying? When my heart and soul
were mine again, unable to control
themselves for longing—who receives me? All run
and shun me, as if I were a skeleton.
Now I myself begin to feel the fear
I inspire. I wish I were a prisoner
again or dead. Speak! Phaedra says my home
was outraged. Who betrayed me? Someone come
and tell me. I have fought for Greece. Will Greece,
sustained by Theseus, give my enemies
asylum in my household? Tell me why
I've no avenger? Is my son a spy?
You will not answer. I must know my fate.
Suspicion chokes me, while I hesitate
and stand here pleading. Wait, let no one stir.
Phaedra shall tell me what has troubled her.

SCENE VI

Hippolytus

HIPPOLYTUS

What now? His anger turns my blood to ice.
Will Phaedra, always uncertain, sacrifice
herself? What will she tell the King? How hot

the air's becoming here! I feel the rot
of love seeping like poison through this house.
I feel the pollution. I cannot rouse
my former loyalties. When I try to gather
the necessary strength to face my father,
my mind spins with some dark presentiment . . .
How can such terror touch the innocent?
I LOVE ARICIA! Father, I confess
my treason to you is my happiness!
I LOVE ARICIA! Will this bring you joy,
our love you have no power to destroy?

ACT 4

SCENE I

Theseus, Oenone

THESEUS

What's this, you tell me he dishonors me,
and has assaulted Phaedra's chastity?
Oh heavy fortune, I no longer know
who loves me, who I am, or where I go.
Who has ever seen such disloyalty
after such love? Such sly audacity!
His youth made no impression on her soul,
so he fell back on force to reach his goal!
I recognize this perjured sword; I gave
him this myself to teach him to be brave!
Oh Zeus, are blood-ties no impediment?

Phaedra tried to save him from punishment!
Why did her silence spare this parricide?

OENONE

She hoped to spare a trusting father's pride.
She felt so sickened by your son's attempt,
his hot eyes leering at her with contempt,
she had no wish to live. She read out her will
to me, then lifted up her arm to kill
herself. I struck the sword out of her hand.
Fainting, she babbled the secret she had planned
to bury with her in the grave. My ears
unwillingly interpreted her tears.

THESEUS

Oh traitor! I know why he seemed to blanch
and toss with terror like an aspen branch
when Phaedra saw him. Now I know why he stood
back, then embraced me so coldly he froze my blood.
Was Athens the first stage for his obscene
attentions? Did he dare attack the Queen
before our marriage?

OENONE

                Remember her disgust
and hate then? She already feared his lust.

THESEUS

And when I sailed, this started up again?

OENONE

I've hidden nothing. Do you want your pain
redoubled? Phaedra calls me. Let me go,
and save her. I have told you what I know.

SCENE II

Theseus, Hippolytus

THESEUS

My son returns! Oh God, reserved and cool,
dressed in a casual freedom that could fool
the sharpest. Is it right his brows should blaze
and dazzle me with virtue's sacred rays?
Are there not signs? Should not ADULTERER
in looping scarlet script be branded there?

HIPPOLYTUS

What cares becloud your kingly countenance,
Father! What is this irritated glance?
Tell me! Are you afraid to trust your son?

THESEUS

How dare you stand here? May the great Zeus stone
me, if I let my fondness and your birth
protect you! Is my strength which rid the earth
of brigands paralysed? Am I so sick
and senile, any coward with a stick
can strike me? Am I a schoolboy's target? Oh God,
am I food for vultures? Some carrion you must prod
and poke to see if it's alive or dead?
Your hands are moist and itching for my bed,
Coward! Wasn't begetting you enough
dishonor to destroy me? Must I snuff
your perjured life, my own son's life, and stain
a thousand glories? Let the gods restrain

my fury! Fly! live hated and alone—
there are places where my name may be unknown.
Go, find them, follow your disastrous star
through filth; if I discover where you are,
I'll add another body to the hill
of vermin I've extinguished by my skill.
Fly from me, let the grieving storm-winds bear
your contagion from me. You corrupt the air.
I call upon Poseidon. Help me, Lord
of Ocean, help your servant! Once my sword
heaped crucified assassins on your shore
and let them burn like beacons. God, you swore
my first request would be fulfilled. My first!
I never made it. Even through the worst
torments of Epirus I held my peace;
no threat or torture brought me to my knees
beseeching favors; even then I knew
some greater project was reserved for you!
Poseidon, now I kneel. Avenge me, dash
my incestuous son against your rocks, and wash
his dishonor from my household; wave on wave
of roaring nothingness shall be his grave.

HIPPOLYTUS

Phaedra accuses me of lawless love!
Phaedra! My heart stops, I can hardly move
my lips and answer. I have no defense,
if you condemn me without evidence.

THESEUS

Oh coward, you were counting on the Queen
to hide your brutal insolence and screen
your outrage with her weakness! You forgot

something. You dropped your sword and spoiled your plot.
You should have kept it. Surely you had time
to kill the only witness to your crime!

HIPPOLYTUS

Why do I stand this, and forbear to clear
away these lies, and let the truth appear?
I could so easily. Where would you be,
if I spoke out? Respect my loyalty,
Father, respect your own intelligence.
Examine me. What am I? My defense
is my whole life. When have I wavered, when
have I pursued the vices of young men?
Father, you have no scaffolding to rig
your charges on. Small crimes precede the big.
Phaedra accused me of attempting rape!
Am I some Proteus, who can change his shape?
Nature despises such disparities.
Vice, like virtue, advances by degrees.
Bred by Antiope to manly arms,
I hate the fever of this lust that warms
the loins and rots the spirit. I was taught
uprightness by Theramenes. I fought
with wolves, tamed horses, gave my soul to sport,
and shunned the joys of women and the court.
I dislike praise, but those who know me best
grant me one virtue—it's that I detest
the very crimes of which I am accused.
How often you yourself have been amused
and puzzled by my love of purity,
pushed to the point of crudeness. By the sea
and in the forests, I have filled my heart
with freedom, far from women.

THESEUS

　　　　　　　When this part
was dropped, could only Phaedra violate
the cold abyss of your immaculate
reptilian soul. How could this funeral urn
contain a heart, a living heart, or burn
for any woman but my wife?

HIPPOLYTUS

　　　　　Ah no!
Father, I too have seen my passions blow
into a tempest. Why should I conceal
my true offense? I feel, Father, I feel
what other young men feel. I love, I love
Aricia. Father, I love the sister of
your worst enemies. I worship her!
I only feel and breathe and live for her!

THESEUS

You love Aricia? God! No, this is meant
to blind my eyes and throw me off the scent.

HIPPOLYTUS

Father, for six months I have done my worst
to kill this passion. You shall be the first
to know . . . You frown still. Nothing can remove
your dark obsession. Father, what will prove
my innocence? I swear by earth and sky,
and nature's solemn, shining majesty. . . .

THESEUS

Oaths and religion are the common cant

of all betrayers. If you wish to taunt
me, find a better prop than blasphemy.

HIPPOLYTUS

All's blasphemy to eyes that cannot see.
Could even Phaedra bear me such ill will?

THESEUS

Phaedra, Phaedra! Name her again, I'll kill
you! My hand's already on my sword.

HIPPOLYTUS

                          Explain
my terms of exile. What do you ordain?

THESEUS

Sail out across the ocean. Everywhere
on earth and under heaven is too near.

HIPPOLYTUS

Who'll take me in? Oh who will pity me,
and give me bread, if you adandon me?

THESEUS

You'll find fitting companions. Look for friends
who honor everything that most offends.
Pimps and jackals who praise adultery
and incest will protect your purity!

HIPPOLYTUS

Adultery! Is it your privilege
to fling this word in my teeth? I've reached the edge
of madness . . . No, I'll say no more. Compare

my breeding with Phaedra's. Think and beware . . .
She had a mother . . . No, I must not speak.

THESEUS

You devil, you'll attack the queen still weak
from your assault. How can you stand and face
your father? Must I drive you from this place
with my own hand. Run off, or I will flog
you with the flat of my sword like a dog!

SCENE III

Theseus

THESEUS

You go to your inevitable fate,
Child—by the river immortals venerate.
Poseidon gave his word. You cannot fly:
death and the gods march on invisibly.
I loved you once; despite your perfidy,
my bowels writhe inside me. Must you die?
Yes; I am in too deep now to draw back.
What son has placed his father on such a rack?
What father groans for such a monstrous birth?
Oh gods, your thunder throws me to the earth.

SCENE IV

Theseus, Phaedra

PHAEDRA

Theseus, I heard the deluge of your voice,
and stand here trembling. If there's time for choice,
hold back your hand, still bloodless; spare your race!
I supplicate you, I kneel here for grace.
Oh, Theseus, Theseus, will you drench the earth
with your own blood? His virtue, youth and birth
cry out for him. Is he already slain
by you for me—spare me this incestuous pain!

THESEUS

Phaedra, my son's blood has not touched my hand;
and yet I'll be avenged. On sea and land,
spirits, the swift of foot, shall track him down.
Poseidon owes me this. Why do you frown?

PHAEDRA

Poseidon owes you this? What have you done
in anger?

THESEUS

What! You wish to help my son?
No, stir my anger, back me to the hilt,
call for blacker colors to paint his guilt.
Lash, strike and drive me on! You cannot guess
the nerve and fury of his wickedness.
Phaedra, he slandered your sincerity,

he told me your accusation was a lie.
He swore he loved Aricia, he wants to wed
Aricia. . . .

PHAEDRA

What, my lord!

THESEUS

That's what he said.
Of course, I scorn his shallow artifice.
Help me, Poseidon, hear me, sacrifice
my son. I seek the altar. Come! Let us both
kneel down and beg the gods to keep their oath.

SCENE V

Phaedra

PHAEDRA

My husband's gone, still rumbling his own name
and fame. He has no inkling of the flame
his words have started. If he hadn't spoken,
I might have . . . I was on my feet, I'd broken
loose from Oenone, and had just begun
to say I know not what to save his son.
Who knows how far I would have gone? Remorse,
longing and anguish shook me with such force,
I might have told the truth and suffered death,
before this revelation stopped my breath:
Hippolytus is not insensible,

only insensible to me! His dull
heart chases shadows. He is glad to rest
upon Aricia's adolescent breast!
Oh thin abstraction! When I saw his firm
repugnance spurn my passion like a worm,
I thought he had some magic to withstand
the lure of any woman in the land,
and now I see a schoolgirl leads the boy,
as simply as her puppy or a toy.
Was I about to perish for this sham,
this panting hypocrite? Perhaps I am
the only woman that he could refuse!

SCENE VI

Phaedra, Oenone

PHAEDRA

Oenone, dearest, have you heard the news?

OENONE

No, I know nothing, but I am afraid.
How can I follow you? You have betrayed
your life and children. What have you revealed,
Madam?

PHAEDRA

      I have a rival in the field,
Oenone.

OENONE

What?

PHAEDRA

Oenone, he's in love—
this howling monster, able to disprove
my beauty, mock my passion, scorn each prayer,
and face me like a tiger in its lair—
he's tamed, the beast is harnessed to a cart;
Aricia's found an entrance to his heart.

OENONE

Aricia?

PHAEDRA

Nurse, my last calamity
has come. This is the bottom of the sea.
All that preceded this had little force—
the flames of lust, the horrors of remorse,
the prim refusal by my grim young master,
were only feeble hints of this disaster.
They love each other! Passion blinded me.
I let them blind me, let them meet and see
each other freely! Was such bounty wrong?
Oenone, you have known this all along,
you must have seen their meetings, watched them sneak
off to their forest, playing hide-and-seek!
Alas, such rendezvous are no offence:
innocent nature smiles of innocence,
for them each natural impulse was allowed,
each day was summer and without a cloud.

Oenone, nature hated me. I fled
its light, as if a price were on my head.
I shut my eyes and hungered for my end.
Death was the only God my vows could bend.
And even while my desolation served
me gall and tears, I knew I was observed;
I never had security or leisure
for honest weeping, but must steal this pleasure.
Oh hideous pomp; a monarch only wears
the robes of majesty to hide her tears!

OENONE

How can their folly help them? They will never
enjoy its fruit.

PHAEDRA

          Ugh, they will love forever—
even while I am talking, they embrace,
they scorn me, they are laughing in my face!
In the teeth of exile, I hear them swear
they will be true forever, everywhere.
Oenone, have pity on my jealous rage;
I'll kill this happiness that jeers at age.
I'll summon Theseus; hate shall answer hate!
I'll drive my husband to annihilate
Aricia—let no trivial punishment,
her instant death, or bloodless banishment . . .
What am I saying? Have I lost my mind?
I am jealous, and call my husband! Bind
me, gag me; I am frothing with desire.
My husband is alive, and I'm on fire!

For whom? Hippolytus. When I have said
his name, blood fills my eyes, my heart stops dead.
Imposture, incest, murder! I have passed
the limits of damnation; now at last,
my lover's lifeblood is my single good.
Nothing else cools my murderous thirst for blood.
Yet I live on! I live, looked down upon
by my progenitor, the sacred sun,
by Zeus, by Europa, by the universe
of gods and stars, my ancestors. They curse
their daughter. Let me die. In the great night
of Hades, I'll find shelter from their sight.
What am I saying? I've no place to turn:
Minos, my father, holds the judge's urn.
The gods have placed damnation in his hands,
the shades in Hades follow his commands.
Will he not shake and curse his fatal star
that brings his daughter trembling to his bar?
His child by Pasiphaë forced to tell
a thousand sins unclassified in hell?
Father, when you interpret what I speak,
I fear your fortitude will be too weak
to hold the urn. I see you fumbling for
new punishments for crimes unknown before.
You'll be your own child's executioner!
You cannot kill me; look, my murderer
is Venus, who destroyed our family;
Father, she has already murdered me.
I killed myself—and what is worse I wasted
my life for pleasures I have never tasted.
My lover flees me still, and my last gasp
is for the fleeting flesh I failed to clasp.

OENONE

Madam, Madam, cast off this groundless terror!
Is love now an unprecedented error?
You love! What then? You love! Accept your fate.
You're not the first to sail into this strait.
Will chaos overturn the earth and Jove,
because a mortal woman is in love?
Such accidents are easy, all too common.
A woman must submit to being woman.
You curse a failure in the source of things.
Venus has feasted on the hearts of kings;
even the gods, man's judges, feel desire,
Zeus learned to live with his adulterous fire.

PHAEDRA

Must I still listen and drink your poisoned breath?
My death's redoubled on the edge of death.
I'd fled Hippolytus and I was free
till your entreaties stabbed and blinded me,
and dragged me howling to the pit of lust.
Oenone, I was learning to be just.
You fed my malice. Attacking the young Prince
was not enough; you clothed him with my sins.
You wished to kill him; he is dying now,
because of you, and Theseus' brutal vow.
You watch my torture; I'm the last ungorged
scrap rotting in this trap your plots have forged.
What binds you to me? Leave me, go, and die,
may your punishment be to terrify
all those who ruin princes by their lies,
hints, acquiescence, filth, and blasphemies—
panders who grease the grooves of inclination,
and lure our willing bodies from salvation.

Go die, go frighten false flatterers, the worst
friends the gods can give to kings they've cursed!

OENONE

I have given all and left all for her service,
almighty gods! I have been paid my price!

ACT 5

SCENE I

Hippolytus, Aricia

ARICIA

Take a stand, speak the truth, if you respect
your father's glory and your life. Protect
yourself! I'm nothing to you. You consent
without a struggle to your banishment.
If you are weary of Aricia, go;
at least do something to prevent the blow
that dooms your honor and existence—both
at a stroke! Your father must recall his oath;
there is time still, but if the truth's concealed,
you offer your accuser a free field.
Speak to your father!

HIPPOLYTUS

I've already said
what's lawful. Shall I point to his soiled bed,
tell Athens how his marriage was foresworn,
make Theseus curse the day that he was born?
My aching heart recoils. I only want
God and Aricia for my confidants.
See how I love you; love makes me confide
in you this horror I have tried to hide
from my own heart. My faith must not be broken;
forget, if possible, what I have spoken.
Ah Princess, if even a whisper slips
past you, it will perjure your pure lips.
God's justice is committed to the cause
of those who love him, and uphold his laws;
sooner or later, heaven itself will rise
in wrath and punish Phaedra's blasphemies.
I must not. If I rip away her mask,
I'll kill my father. Give me what I ask.
Do this! Then throw away your chains; it's right
for you to follow me, and share my flight.
Fly from this prison; here the vices seethe
and simmer, virtue has no air to breathe.
In the confusion of my exile, none
will even notice that Aricia's gone.
Banished and broken, Princess, I am still
a force in Greece. Your guards obey my will,
powerful intercessors wish us well:
our neighbors, Argos' citadel
is armed, and in Mycenae our allies
will shelter us, if lying Phaedra tries
to hurry us from our paternal throne,

and steal our sacred titles for her son.
The gods are ours, they urge us to attack.
Why do you tremble, falter and hold back?
Your interests drive me to this sacrifice.
While I'm on fire, your blood has changed to ice.
Princess, is exile more than you can face?

ARICIA

Exile with you, my lord? What sweeter place
is under heaven? Standing at your side,
I'd let the universe and heaven slide.
You're my one love, my king, but can I hope
for peace and honor, Prince, if I elope
unmarried? This . . . I wasn't questioning
the decency of flying from the King.
Is he my father? Only an abject
spirit honors tyrants with respect.
You say you love me. Prince, I am afraid.

HIPPOLYTUS

Aricia, you shall never be betrayed;
accept me! Let our love be sanctified,
then flee from your oppressor as my bride.
Bear witness, oh you gods, our love released
by danger, needs no temple or a priest.
It's faith, not ceremonial, that saves.
Here at the city gates, among these graves
the resting places of my ancient line,
there stands a sacred temple and a shrine.
Here, where no mortal ever swore in vain,
here in these shadows, where eternal pain
is ready to engulf the perjurer;
here heaven's scepter quivers to confer

its final sanction; here, my Love, we'll kneel,
and pray the gods to consecrate and seal
our love. Zeus, the father of the world will stand
here as your father and bestow your hand.
Only the pure shall be our witnesses:
Hera, the guarantor of marriages,
Demeter and the virgin Artemis.

ARICIA

The King is coming. Fly. I'll stay and meet
his anger here and cover your retreat.
Hurry. Be off, send me some friend to guide
my timid footsteps, husband, to your side.

SCENE II

Theseus, Ismene, Aricia

THESEUS

Oh God, illuminate my troubled mind.
Show me the answer I have failed to find.

ARICIA

Go, Ismene, be ready to escape.

SCENE III

Theseus, Aricia

THESEUS

Princess, you are disturbed. You twist your cape
and blush. The Prince was talking to you. Why
is he running?

ARICIA

We've said our last goodbye,
my lord.

THESEUS

I see the beauty of your eyes
moves even my son, and you have gained a prize
no woman hoped for.

ARICIA

He hasn't taken on
your hatred for me, though he is your son.

THESEUS

I follow. I can hear the oaths he swore.
He knelt, he wept. He has done this before
and worse. You are deceived.

ARICIA

Deceived, my lord?

THESEUS

Princess, are you so rich? Can you afford

to hunger for this lover that my queen
rejected? Your betrayer loves my wife.

ARICIA

How can you bear to blacken his pure life?
Is kingship only for the blind and strong,
unable to distinguish right from wrong?
What insolent prerogative obscures
a light that shines in every eye but yours?
You have betrayed him to his enemies.
What more, my lord? Repent your blasphemies.
Are you not fearful lest the gods so loathe
and hate you they will gratify your oath?
Fear God, my lord, fear God. How many times
he grants men's wishes to expose their crimes.

THESEUS

Love blinds you, Princess, and beclouds your reason.
Your outburst cannot cover up his treason.
My trust's in witnesses that cannot lie.
I have seen Phaedra's tears. She tried to die.

ARICIA

Take care, your Highness. What your killing hand
drove all the thieves and reptiles from the land,
you missed one monster, one was left alive,
one . . . No, I must not name her, Sire, or strive
to save your helpless son; he wants to spare
your reputation. Let me go. I dare
not stay here. If I stayed I'd be too weak
to keep my promise. I'd be forced to speak.

SCENE IV

Theseus

THESEUS

What was she saying? I must try to reach
the meaning of her interrupted speech.
Is it a pitfall? A conspiracy?
Are they plotting together to torture me?
Why did I let the rash, wild girl depart?
What is this whisper crying in my heart?
A secret pity fills my soul with pain.
I must question Oenone once again.
My guards, summon Oenone to the throne.
Quick, bring her. I must talk with her alone.

SCENE V

Theseus, Panope

PANOPE

The Queen's deranged, your Highness. Some accursed
madness is driving her; some fury stalks
behind her back, possesses her, and talks
its evil through her, and blasphemes the world.
She cursed Oenone. Now Oenone's hurled
herself into the ocean, Sire, and drowned.
Why did she do it. No reason can be found.

THESEUS

Oenone's drowned?

PANOPE

Her death has brought no peace.
The cries of Phaedra's troubled soul increase.
Now driven by some sinister unrest,
she snatches up her children to her breast,
pets them and weeps, till something makes her scoff
at her affection, and she drives them off.
Her glance is drunken and irregular,
she looks through us and wonders who we are;
thrice she has started letters to you, Sire,
thrice tossed the shredded fragments in the fire.
Oh call her to you. Help her!

THESEUS

The nurse is drowned? Phaedra wishes to die?
Oh gods! Summon my son. Let him defend
himself, tell him I'm ready to attend.
I want him!

Exit Panope

Neptune, hear me, spare my son!
My vengeance was too hastily begun.
Oh why was I so eager to believe
Oenone's accusation? The gods deceive
the victims they are ready to destroy!

SCENE VI

Theseus, Theramenes

THESEUS

Here is Theramenes. Where is my boy,
my first-born? He was yours to guard and keep.
Where is he? Answer me. What's this? You weep?

THERAMENES

Oh, tardy, futile grief, his blood is shed.
My lord, your son, Hippolytus, is dead.

THESEUS

Oh gods, have mercy!

THERAMENES

        I saw him die. The most
lovely and innocent of men is lost.

THESEUS

He's dead? The gods have hurried him away
and killed him? . . . just as I began to pray . . .
What sudden thunderbolt has struck him down?

THERAMENES

We'd started out, and hardly left the town.
He held the reins; a few feet to his rear,
a single, silent guard held up a spear.
He followed the Mycenae highroad, deep
in thought, reins dangling, as if half asleep;

his famous horses, only he could hold,
trudged on with lowered heads, and sometimes rolled
their dull eyes slowly—they seemed to have caught
their master's melancholy, and aped his thought.
Then all at once winds struck us like a fist,
we heard a sudden roaring through the mist;
from underground a voice in agony
answered the prolonged groaning of the sea.
We shook, the horses' manes rose on their heads,
and now against a sky of blacks and reds,
we saw the flat waves hump into a mountain
of green-white water rising like a fountain,
as it reached land and crashed with a last roar
to shatter like a galley on the shore.
Out of its fragments rose a monster, half
dragon, half bull; a mouth that seemed to laugh
drooled venom on its dirty yellow scales
and python belly, forking to three tails.
The shore was shaken like a tuning fork,
ships bounced on the stung sea like bits of cork,
the earth moved, and the sun spun round and round,
a sulphur-colored venom swept the ground.
We fled; each felt his useless courage falter,
and sought asylum at a nearby altar.
Only the Prince remained; he wheeled about,
and hurled a javelin through the monster's snout.
Each kept advancing. Flung from the Prince's arm,
dart after dart struck where the blood was warm.
The monster in its death-throes felt defeat,
and bounded howling to the horses' feet.
There its stretched gullet and its armor broke,
and drenched the chariot with blood and smoke,
and then the horses, terror-struck, stampeded.

Their master's whip and shouting went unheeded,
they dragged his breathless body to the spray.
Their red mouths bit the bloody surf, men say
Poseidon stood beside them, that the god
was stabbing at their bellies with a goad.
Their terror drove them crashing on a cliff,
the chariot crashed in two, they ran as if
the Furies screamed and crackled in their manes,
their fallen hero tangled in the reins,
jounced on the rocks behind them. The sweet light
of heaven never will expunge this sight:
the horses that Hippolytus had tamed,
now dragged him headlong, and their mad hooves maimed
his face past recognition. When he tried
to call them, calling only terrified;
faster and ever faster moved their feet,
his body was a piece of bloody meat.
The cliffs and ocean trembled to our shout,
at last their panic failed, they turned about,
and stopped not far from where those hallowed graves,
the Prince's fathers, overlook the waves.
I ran on breathless, guards were at my back,
my master's blood had left a generous track.
The stones were red, each thistle in the mud
was stuck with bits of hair and skin and blood.
I came upon him, called; he stretched his right
hand to me, blinked his eyes, then closed them tight.
"I die," he whispered, "it's the gods' desire.
Friend, stand between Aricia and my sire—
some day enlightened, softened, disabused,
he will lament his son, falsely accused;
then when at last he wishes to appease
my soul, he'll treat my lover well, release

and honor Aricia. . . ." On this word, he died.
Only a broken body testified
he'd lived and loved once. On the sand now lies
something his father will not recognize.

THESEUS

My son, my son! Alas, I stand alone
before the gods. I never can atone.

THERAMENES

Meanwhile Aricia, rushing down the path,
approached us. She was fleeing from your wrath,
my lord, and wished to make Hippolytus
her husband in God's eyes. Then nearing us,
she saw the signs of struggle in the waste,
she saw (oh what a sight) her love defaced,
her young love lying lifeless on the sand.
At first she hardly seemed to understand;
while staring at the body in the grass,
she kept on asking where her lover was.
At last the black and fearful truth broke through
her desolation! She seemed to curse the blue
and murdering ocean, as she caught his head
up in her lap; then fainting lay half dead,
until Ismene somehow summoned back her breath,
restored the child to life—or rather death.
I come, great King, to urge my final task,
your dying son's last outcry was to ask
mercy for poor Aricia, for his bride.
Now Phaedra comes. She killed him. She has lied.

SCENE VII

Theseus, Phaedra, Panope

THESEUS

Ah Phaedra, you have won. He's dead. A man
was killed. Were you watching? His horses ran
him down, and tore his body limb from limb.
Poseidon struck him, Theseus murdered him.
I served you! Tell me why Oenone died?
Was it to save you? Is her suicide
A proof of your truth? No, since he's dead, I must
accept your evidence, just or unjust.
I must believe my faith has been abused;
you have accused him; he shall stand accused.
He's friendless even in the world below.
There the shades fear him! Am I forced to know
the truth? Truth cannot bring my son to life.
If fathers murder, shall I kill my wife
too? Leave me, Phaedra. Far from you, exiled
from Greece, I will lament my murdered child.
I am a murdered gladiator, whirled
in black circles. I want to leave the world;
my whole life rises to increase my guilt—
all those dazzled, dazzling eyes, my glory built
on killing killers. Less known, less magnified,
I might escape, and find a place to hide.
Stand back, Poseidon. I know the gods are hard
to please. I pleased you. This is my reward:
I killed my son. I killed him! Only a god
spares enemies, and wants his servants' blood!

PHAEDRA

No, Theseus, I must disobey your prayer.
Listen to me. I'm dying. I declare
Hippolytus was innocent.

THESEUS

Ah Phaedra, on your evidence, I sent
him to his death. Do you ask me to forgive
my son's assassin? Can I let you live?

PHAEDRA

My time's too short, your highness. It was I,
who lusted for your son with my hot eye.
The flames of Aphrodite maddened me;
I loathed myself, and yearned outrageously
like a starved wolf to fall upon the sheep.
I wished to hold him to me in my sleep
and dreamt I had him. Then Oenone's tears,
troubled my mind; she played upon my fears,
until her pleading forced me to declare
I loved your son. He scorned me. In despair,
I plotted with my nurse, and our conspiracy
made you believe your son assaulted me.
Oenone's punished; fleeing from my wrath,
she drowned herself, and found a too easy path
to death and hell. Perhaps you wonder why
I still survive her, and refuse to die?
Theseus, I stand before you to absolve
your noble son. Sire, only this resolve
upheld me, and made me throw down my knife.
I've chosen a slower way to end my life—
Medea's poison; chills already dart
along my boiling veins and squeeze my heart.

A cold composure I have never known
gives me a moment's poise. I stand alone
and seem to see my outraged husband fade
and waver into death's dissolving shade.
My eyes at last give up their light, and see
the day they've soiled resume its purity.

PANOPE

She's dead, my lord.

THESEUS

       Would God, all memory
of her and me had died with her! Now I
must live. This knowledge that has come too late
must give me strength and help me expiate
my sacrilegious vow. Let's go, I'll pay
my son the honors he has earned today.
His father's tears shall mingle with his blood.
My love that did my son so little good
asks mercy from his spirit. I declare
Aricia is my daughter and my heir.

FIGARO'S
MARRIAGE

PREFACE

In Flaubert's *Dictionary of Accepted Ideas* the entry under "Figaro, Marriage of" runs: "Another of the causes of the French Revolution." This tells us that less than a hundred years after Beaumarchais's play, the character of the scheming and impudent valet had come to be regarded as the prototype of emancipated modern man. Though wearing silk breeches, Figaro was taken as a liberal bourgeois of 1840 who was ahead of his time. Vague recollections of the story that, when the comedy was first produced in 1784, a countess was struck by a half-eaten apple thrown from the pit, combined with the famous attack on rank and privilege in Act V to clinch the conclusion that Beaumarchais had written an egalitarian tract.

But whoever takes the trouble to read the work finds that it differs from this description almost as much as it does from Mozart's opera. In the first place, the role of the scheming and impudent valet, far from being new and political, is traditional and purely comic. The very name Figaro, which is probably a corruption of *picaro,* suggests the familiar hero of innumerable novels: a wanderer living by his wits and whose adventures uncover the seamy side of high life.

Beaumarchais, who was a great schemer and a self-made man, clearly enjoyed plotting as an end in itself, and he carried it so far in this second Figaro comedy that he thought it necessary for credibility to call it "One Mad Day." We should remember, also, that in *The Barber of Seville,* which comes before, Figaro deploys his genius in aid of Count Almaviva's passion for Rosine as in the *Marriage* he serves his own for Suzanne. None of this suggests revolution. Rather, it suggests the primacy of love. This love is an urbane, intelligent, well-schooled feeling, which turns sentimental only in the few moments when the idea of motherhood is introduced by the recognition of Marceline. Otherwise, love à la Beaumarchais is naïve and delicate in Fanchette and Cherubino, restless yet controlled in the Count, frank but domestic in Figaro, and touchingly dignified—just short of pathetic—in the Countess.

Without paradox, all these loves are *manly.* They have character and are attractive to see. They reflect and presuppose an aristocratic society. One cannot conceive without leisure and wealth so much witty observation upon feeling and so much freedom in action. Figaro and Suzanne run risks, it is true, but when they are not deliberately defying the Count their behavior denotes a habit of independence which is not that of the rebellious declaimer we find in the two great soliloquies.

In those two speeches Beaumarchais meant to condense at once his satire and his resentments, and he succeeded so well that it is this disaffected, sardonic Figaro who is remembered as the hero of the double intrigue and a cause of the French Revolution. The truth is that Figaro's ideas about society were hardly new, except on the stage, when they appeared there in 1784. Thanks to the "liberals" of a century before, to Montesquieu and Voltaire, to Diderot and The Encyclopedists, thanks above all to Rousseau's writings and personality, the enlightened aristocracy and high bourgeoisie of the eighteenth century were quite convinced that birth was worthless compared to talents and that established authority cloaked incompetence and injustice. A theatrical audience could respond to Figaro's indignation because it seemed not so much subversive as appropriate.

And like his audience Beaumarchais favored a very special kind of reform, the kind we shall never see: he wanted merit rewarded. His aristocracy was that of talents and virtues sustained by the impartial administration of just laws. No more than his idol Voltaire did he want a whitewash of equality that would give Basil and Bartholo an even greater chance to indulge their malice. As for liberty, it is clear he wanted it safeguarded from both the power of money and the envy of mean souls. It would have damped even his sanguine spirits to know that the first newspaper to take the name Figaro, in the 1850's, specialized in sneers and abuse against whatever was high-minded and nobly ambitious in French letters, art, and public life. Beaumarchais's Figaro was a gentleman by instinct and a cynic only for the instruction of the pit. As Marceline says: "He is always cheerful and oh! so generous!"

And now a word about translation. I know of no works more difficult to turn from French into English than the plays of Beaumarchais. The author was a great jumping wit, and he delighted in making his audience jump as well, for its own pleasure. In *Figaro* the "retortive backchat"—to use Shaw's definition of dramatic dialogue—surpasses in rapidity and allusiveness that in *The Barber of Seville* or in any other French comedy of the century.

It follows that even an accurate translation of the words and the meaning may still leave *the point* unexpressed. When this happens it makes Beaumarchais sound incoherent, as if he were a modern exploring the unconscious and its random associations, instead of a man of the ratiocinative century, in which the mainspring of amusement, intrigue, and conversation alike was to witness diverse interests intently pursued, which nevertheless converge in a common situation.

I am not at all confident that for every difficult speech in a play that has few of any other kind I have provided an equivalent that matches the original in its two main aspects—that which is meant for the previous speaker and that which addresses the audience. But supposing this achieved, there remains the problem of tone. Beaumarchais's idiomatic simplicity rarely drops into crude colloquialism, yet it observes the differences within the common tongue spoken by a nobleman and his wife, by a judge and a doctor, and by servants and others of various ranks and degrees of education. Moreover, Figaro and Suzanne, and sometimes the Count and his Countess, employ two distinct modes of expression, depending on whether they are giving spontaneous answers or "making a speech." Indeed, the heterogeneous language of the play is of all elements the one true harbinger of social revolution —which does not prevent the author from indulging his gift of graceful phrasing, rapid but clear, highly organized but sayable. By attempting to provide these things in proportional measure, I have meant to break new ground, for the versions of *Figaro* that I have chanced to read, in manuscript or print, are, in detail and as wholes, travesties of the play.

But to give something better than journeyman work, out of devotion to Beaumarchais and deference to two great languages, has required some compromises. Once or twice I have ventured to change the author's meaning, without (I hope) changing his intention. For example, references to "the torrent of the Morena" and to the Guadalquivir river are here rendered as "mountain torrent" and "nearest fishpond," these being the clichés suitable to the occasion. Enough foreignness is left in the several mentions of

Andalusia, the Spanish Empire, Catalonia, and the honor of a Castilian nobleman, to parallel Beaumarchais's pretense of local atmosphere. I have also changed the horse-chestnut trees in Acts IV and V to elms, for obvious reasons that the reader will discover and can hardly fail to approve.

A more important change was that imposed by the need to make plausible and entertaining the great legal quibble in Act III. The French equivocates on the words *ou* and *où*. I had to tamper slightly with two speeches to do something comparable.

Again, recognizing in Beaumarchais the originator of modern stage directions, which instruct the actor in his interpretation and costuming, I wanted to include in my version the character descriptions the author prefixed to the printed play. Among these, several are set down as "the same as in *The Barber of Seville*." I have therefore lifted a few lines from the author's edition of *The Barber* and inserted them in the appropriate places.

The present English version, in short, is for the reader, the actor, and the director. It is scrupulous, but it is not a text for research scholars and even less a trot for schoolboys: the former would be led astray about minutiae and the latter would earn very poor marks. But I entertain the hope that if in his present abode Beaumarchais has learned more English than his "God damn" of 1784, he will bestow an indulgent approval on my effort to reproduce his feelings and fireworks in a tongue other than the one he handled so discouragingly well.

JACQUES BARZUN

CHARACTERS AND COSTUMING

COUNT ALMAVIVA (Governor of Andalusia) must be played with nobility of mien, but also with lightness and ease. The corruption of his heart must not diminish the perfect good form of his manners. In keeping with the morals *of those days,* the great regarded the conquest of women as a frolic. This role is an uncomfortable one in that its grandeur is invariably brought down and sacrificed to the other characters. But in the hands of a good actor the role can bring out all the others and insure the success of the piece.

In the first and second acts the Count wears a hunting costume in the old Spanish style with half-length boots. In the remaining acts he wears a more gorgeous version of the same costume.

COUNTESS ALMAVIVA, who is moved by two opposite feelings, must show only a restrained tenderness and a moderate anger. Nothing must lower in the spectator's eyes her virtuous and lovable character. This role is one of the most difficult in the play.

The Countess's costume in the first, second, third, and fourth acts consists of a comfortable house coat of straight and simple lines. She wears no ornament on her head. She is supposed to be indisposed and keeping to her room. In the fifth act she wears Suzanne's clothes and the high hairdress that goes with them.

FIGARO (valet to the Count and steward of the castle). The actor who plays this role cannot be too strongly urged to study and make prevail at all times the true spirit of the character. If the actor finds in the part nothing but argumentativeness spiced with gaiety and wit; or even worse, if he allows himself any burlesquing, he will debase a role with which the greatest comedian can do himself honor by seizing upon its many nuances and sustaining the highest possibilities of its conception.

Figaro's clothes are the same as in *The Barber of Seville,* that is, the suit of a Spanish majordomo. On his hair he wears a net; his hat is white and has a colored ribbon around the crown. A silk scarf is loosely tied around his neck. His vest and breeches are of satin with buttons and buttonholes finished in silver. His silk sash is very broad, his garters tied with cord and tassels which hang down on the leg. His coat must be of a color contrasting with the vest, but the lapels match the latter. White stockings and gray shoes.

SUZANNE (chief chambermaid to the Countess). A clever girl, full of wit and laughter, but displaying nothing of the impudent frivolity of our corruptive chambermaids. In her role, though it is nearly the longest in the play, there is not a word that is not inspired by goodness and devotion to her duty. The only trickery she allows herself is in behalf of her mistress, who relies on Suzanne's attachment and who has herself none but honorable thoughts.

Suzanne's costume in the first four acts is a tight bodice with flounced skirt, elegant though modeled on the peasant style. Her hat is a high toque (later called in France à la Suzanne). In the festivities of Act IV, the Count places on her head a white toque adorned with a long veil, tall feathers, and ribbons. In Act V she wears the Countess's house coat and nothing on her head.

MARCELINE (housekeeper in the castle) is an intelligent woman with lively instincts, whose experiences and mistakes have amended her character. If the actress who plays the role can rise with a certain judicious pride to the high morality that follows the recognition scene in Act III, it will add greatly to the interest of the play.

Her costume is that of the Spanish duenna, modest in color, a black bonnet on the head.

ANTONIO (a gardener, uncle of Suzanne and father of Fanchette) must display only a half-tipsy condition, which gradually wears off, so that by Act V it is almost unnoticeable.

His clothes are those of a Spanish peasant; the sleeves hang down behind; a hat and white shoes.

FANCHETTE (the daughter of Antonio) is a girl of twelve and very naïve. Her costume has a tight-fitting bodice, peasant style, brown with silver buttons. The skirt is of contrasting color. She wears a black toque with feathers. The other girls in the wedding party are dressed like her.

CHERUBINO (chief page to the Count). This role cannot be properly played except by a young and very pretty woman. There is no young man on our stage who is sufficiently educated to feel the subtleties of the part. Excessively shy before the Countess, he is elsewhere a charmingly naughty boy. A vague restless desire is at the root of his character. He is rushing headlong through adolescence, but aimlessly and without worldly knowledge; he is the plaything of each passing event. In short, he is probably what every mother would like her son to be, even when she knows she will suffer for it.

In the first and second acts, Cherubino's costume is the rich court dress of a Spanish page, white trimmed with silver lace. He wears a light blue cloak off the shoulder and a hat with large plumes. In Act IV, he wears the bodice, skirt and toque of the peasant girls; in Act V, an officer's uniform, a sword, and a cockade.

BARTHOLO (a doctor from Seville). His character and costume are the same as in the *Barber of Seville,* that is, a short, black gown, buttoned up to the neck, and a large wig. The collar and cuffs are turned back and the belt is black. Outdoors he wears a long scarlet coat. In the present play, his role is secondary.

BASIL (the Countess's music master). Also secondary, Basil's character and costume are the same as in *The Barber,* which is to say: a black hat with hanging brim, a gown like a cassock and a long coat without turned-up collar or cuffs.

DON GUZMAN BRIDLEGOOSE (Associate Justice of the district). He must have the open and easy self-assurance of an animal that has overcome its shyness. His stammer is only an additional charm, scarcely noticeable though it is. The performer would make a grave mistake to stress the ludicrous in this part, for the principle of it is the natural contrast between the solemnity of his office and the absurdity of his person. Therefore the less the actor burlesques the man, the more truly will the character appear and the actor's talent shine.

The costume is the robe of a Spanish judge, but less full than that of our state's attorneys—it is almost a cassock. He wears a great wig and a neckband Spanish style, and he carries a long white wand.

DOUBLEFIST (clerk and secretary to Bridlegoose). He is dressed like the justice, but carries a shorter wand.

THE BEADLE or alguazil wears a coat and carries at his side a sword with a leather guard, but without a leather belt. Not boots but shoes, which are black. A white curly wig and a short white wand.

SUNSTRUCK (a young shepherd) wears peasant clothes, sleeves hanging down, bright colored coat, white hat.

A YOUNG SHEPHERDESS—dressed like Fanchette.

PETER (the Count's postilion). Short belted coat over a vest, a courier's boots, hat and whip, a net over his hair.

Walk-on Parts (valets and peasants)—Some in judge's costume, others dressed as peasants, the rest in livery.

ACT 1

The scene is a half-furnished room. An invalid chair is in the middle. FIGARO *is measuring the floor with a yardstick.* SUZANNE, *in front of a mirror, is fixing in her hair the sprig of orange blossoms commonly called "the bride's bonnet."*

FIGARO Nineteen feet by twenty-six.

SUZANNE Look, Figaro—my bonnet. Do you like it better now?

FIGARO (*taking both her hands in his*) Infinitely better, my sweet. My, what that bunch of flowers—so pretty, so virginal, so suited to the head of a lovely girl—does to a lover on the morning of his wedding!

SUZANNE (*leaving*) What are you measuring there, my lad?

FIGARO I am finding out, dear Suzy, whether the beautiful big bed that his lordship is giving us will fit into this room.

SUZANNE *This* room?

FIGARO He's letting us have it.

SUZANNE But I don't want it.

FIGARO   Why not?

SUZANNE   I don't want it.

FIGARO   But tell me why.

SUZANNE   I don't like it.

FIGARO   You might give a reason.

SUZANNE   And supposing I don't?

FIGARO   Women! As soon as they have us tied down—

SUZANNE   To give a reason would imply that I might be unreasonable. Are you with me or against me?

FIGARO   You are turning down the most convenient room in the castle. It connects with both suites. At night, if my lady is unwell and wants you, she rings—and crack! there you are in two hops. Is it something that my lord requires? a tinkle from his side, and zing! I am at the ready in three strides.

SUZANNE   Right enough! But when he's tinkled in the morning and given you a good long errand, zing! in three strides he is at my door, and crack! in two hops he—

FIGARO   What do you mean by those words?

SUZANNE   You'd better listen to me carefully.

FIGARO   What the devil is going on?

SUZANNE   What is going on is that his lordship Count Almaviva is tired of pursuing the beauties of the neighborhood and is heading for home—not to *his* wife, you understand, but to yours. *She* is the one he has his eye on, and he hopes this apartment will favor his plans. And that is what the faithful Basil, the trusted agent of the Count's pleasures, and my noble singing master as well, tells me every day during my lesson.

FIGARO   Basil, my boy, if ever the application of green birch to an ailing back has helped to correct curvature of the spine, I will—

SUZANNE   So in your innocence you thought that this dowry the Count is giving me was for your beaux yeux and your high merit?

FIGARO   I've done enough to hope it was.

SUZANNE   How stupid bright people are!

FIGARO So they say.

SUZANNE But *they* won't believe it!

FIGARO *They* are wrong.

SUZANNE Get it into your head that the dowry is to get from me, privately, a certain privilege which formerly was the right of the lord of the manor—you know what a grievous right it was.*

FIGARO I know it so well that if the Count had not abolished its shameful exercise when he himself was married, I should never have planned to marry you on his lands.

SUZANNE He abolished it right enough, but he has had second thoughts. And he's thinking your fiancée is the one to restore it to him.

FIGARO (*rubbing his forehead*) My head grows mushy with surprise and my sprouting forehead—**

SUZANNE Please don't rub it.

FIGARO What's the harm?

SUZANNE If you brought on a little pimple, superstitious people might—

FIGARO You're laughing at me, you slut. Now if I could think of some way to catch out this professional deceiver, turn the tables on him and pocket his money—

SUZANNE Plotting and pocketing—you're in your element.

FIGARO It certainly isn't shame that holds me back.

SUZANNE Fear, then?

FIGARO It's no great feat to start on a dangerous undertaking; the thing is to succeed and avoid trouble. Any knavish fool can go into a man's house at night, enjoy his wife, and get a beating for his pains—nothing is easier. But—(*a bell rings*)

SUZANNE My lady is awake. She wanted me to be sure and be the first to talk to her this morning about the wedding.

* This supposed right to enjoy the bride on the wedding night of any vassal is without foundation in law or history, but was widely believed in by the anti-medieval writers.

** The play contains several allusions to the horns of the cuckold, expressed by references to the forehead.

FIGARO Some more goings-on?

SUZANNE The almanac says it brings good luck to forsaken wives. Goodbye Fi-fi-garo, darling; think about ways and means.

FIGARO To prime my brains give a little kiss.

SUZANNE To a lover, today? No sir! What would my husband say tomorrow?

(FIGARO *kisses her*).

SUZANNE Now, now!

FIGARO You don't know how much I love you.

SUZANNE (*adjusting her dress*) When will you learn not to bore me with it from morning till night?

FIGARO (*as if telling a secret*) Why, when I can prove it to you from night till morning.

(*The bell rings again*).

SUZANNE (*blowing him a kiss from the door*) There's your kiss, sir, I have nothing else of yours to return.

FIGARO (*running after her*) But you didn't receive mine across the void like this.

(*Exit* SUZANNE).

FIGARO (*alone*) What a ravishing girl! Always gay, laughing, full of sap, wit, love, joy—and how well-behaved! (*He walks about briskly, rubbing his hands*). Ah, my lord, my dear lord! You want to give me—something to remember? I was wondering, too, why I am first made Steward, and then supposed to become part of the embassy and serve as King's Messenger. Now I understand, Your Excellency: three promotions at one stroke—you as envoy plenipotentiary; myself as political lightning-rod; and Suzy as lady in residence, as private ambassadress—and then, Sir Messenger, be off! While I gallop in one direction, you will drive my girl a long way in the other. While I wade through mud and break my neck for the glory of your family, you will collaborate in the increase of mine. What sweet reciprocity! But, my lord, there is excess in this. To carry on in London the business at once of the

King your master and of your humble servant, to represent in a foreign court both him and me—that is too much by half, much too much. As for you, Basil, my pretty scoundrel, I will teach you to limp with the halt and the lame. I will—no! We must play up to both of them if we are to knock their heads together. Now Figaro, concentrate on today. First, move ahead the time for the wedding, so as to make sure the knot is tied; then distract old Marceline, who is too fond of you; pick up whatever money and gifts there may be; mislead the Count and his little appetites; give a sound drubbing to Mister Basil, and—well, well, well, here is the fat doctor! The party is complete. (*Enter Bartholo and Marceline*) Good-morning, dear doctor of my heart. Is it my wedding with Suzy that brings you to the house?

BARTHOLO (*disdainful*)   Not at all, my dear sir.

FIGARO   It would indeed be a generous act.

BARTHOLO   Exactly, and therefore inconceivably stupid.

FIGARO   It was my bad luck that I had to thwart your designs.*

BARTHOLO   Haven't you anything else to say?

FIGARO   Perhaps your mule hasn't been looked after? *

BARTHOLO (*furious*)   Confounded babbler, leave us alone!

FIGARO   You are angry, doctor? Yours is a cruel profession: no more kindness to animals than if they were men. Farewell, Marceline, are you still thinking of suing me at law? "Though thou love not, must thou therefore hate?" ** I put it to the doctor.

BARTHOLO   What is all this about?

FIGARO (*leaving*)   She will tell you. (*Exit*)

BARTHOLO (*looking at the departing* FIGARO)   The fellow never improves. If someone doesn't flog him alive he will die inside the skin of the most conceited ass I know.

MARCELINE (*attracting his attention*)   Well, here you are at last,

---

* An allusion to the events of *The Barber of Seville,* in which Figaro helped the Count to marry Rosine, the ward of Bartholo, who had himself planned to marry her. Rosine is now Countess Almaviva.
** A line from Voltaire's *Nanine.*

Doctor Ubiquitous,—you always so grave and respectable that one could die waiting for your help, just as some time back someone got married despite your efforts.*

BARTHOLO   And you—always bitter and provoking. But why am I needed here so urgently? Has the Count met with an accident?

MARCELINE   No, doctor.

BARTHOLO   And Rosine, his conspiring countess, could she be— God be praised—unwell?

MARCELINE   She is pining away.

BARTHOLO   What about?

MARCELINE   Her husband neglects her.

BARTHOLO (*with great satisfaction*)   Ah, worthy husband, my avenger!

MARCELINE   It is hard to make out the Count: at once jealous and a philanderer.

BARTHOLO   A philanderer from boredom and jealous from vanity —it's clear as day.

MARCELINE   Today, for example, he is marrying off our Suzanne to Figaro, on whom he lavishes gifts in honor of this union . . .

BARTHOLO   Which His Excellency has made necessary?

MARCELINE   Not quite; but which His Excellency would like to celebrate in secret with the bride . . .

BARTHOLO   Of Mr. Figaro? That's an arrangement the latter is surely willing to enter into.

MARCELINE   Basil is sure it is not so.

BARTHOLO   That other lout lives here too? It's a regular den. What does he do?

MARCELINE   All the evil he can. The worst is the hopeless passion he has so long nursed for me.

BARTHOLO   In your place I should have disposed of that for good.

---

* Another allusion to the events of *The Barber of Seville,* in which Figaro helped the Count to marry Rosine, the ward of Bartholo, who had himself planned to marry her.

MARCELINE How?

BARTHOLO By marrying him.

MARCELINE Tiresome, brutish wit! Why don't you dispose of mine in the same way? You're in honor bound—remember all your promises—and also our little Emmanuel, the offspring of a forgotten love, who was to lead us to the altar.

BARTHOLO Was it to listen to this rigmarole that you had me come from Seville? —What is this fit of marrying you've suddenly fallen into?

MARCELINE We'll say no more about it. But at least help me to marry someone else.

BARTHOLO Gladly. But what mortal, bereft of heaven and women's favors, would . . .

MARCELINE Now, who *could* it be, doctor, but the gay, handsome, lovable Figaro!

BARTHOLO That good-for-nothing?

MARCELINE Never cross, always good-humored, always ready to enjoy the passing moment, worrying as little about the future as about the past—attractive, generous, oh generous! . . .

BARTHOLO . . . as a scamp . . .

MARCELINE . . . as a lord. Delightful, in short. But he is a monster too.

BARTHOLO What about his Suzanne?

MARCELINE She'd never get him, clever as she is, if you would help me, dear doctor, and hold him to a promissory note of his that I have.

BARTHOLO On his wedding day?

MARCELINE Weddings have gone farther than this and been broken off. If I didn't mind giving away a feminine secret—

BARTHOLO There aren't any secrets for a physician.

MARCELINE You know very well I have no secrets from you. Well, our sex is ardent but shy. A certain attraction may draw us toward pleasure, yet the most adventurous woman will say to herself—

"Be beautiful if you can, sensible if you will, but stay respectable: you must!" Now since every woman knows what reputation is worth, we can scare off Suzanne by threatening to expose the offers that are being made to her.

BARTHOLO What will that accomplish?

MARCELINE Just this: ashamed and apprehensive, she will keep on refusing the Count. He, from spite, will support my opposition to her marriage, and hence mine will become a certainty.

BARTHOLO She's right, by God! It's an excellent trick to marry off my old housekeeper to the scoundrel who pinched my young protégée . . .

MARCELINE (*quickly*) . . . the man who plans to serve his pleasure and disappoint my hopes . . .

BARTHOLO . . . the man who once upon a time swindled me out of a hundred pounds that I haven't forgotten.

MARCELINE Ah what bliss!—

BARTHOLO To punish a swindler!—

MARCELINE To marry him, doctor, to marry him!

(*Enter* SUZANNE).

SUZANNE (*holding a bonnet with large ribbons and a woman's dress over her arm*) To marry? To marry whom? My Figaro?

MARCELINE (*sourly*) Why not? Aren't you thinking of it yourself?

BARTHOLO (*laughing*) An angry woman's typical argument! We were speaking, Suzanne my dear, of his happiness in possessing you.

MARCELINE To say nothing of my lord besides.

SUZANNE (*with a curtsy*) Your servant, madam. There is always a touch of gall in your remarks.

MARCELINE (*curtsying*) Your servant as well, madam. Where is the gall? Isn't it justice that a free-handed nobleman share a little in the good things he procures for his people?

SUZANNE He procures?

MARCELINE Yes, madam.

SUZANNE Fortunately, your jealousy is as well known as your claims on Figaro are slight.

MARCELINE They could have been strengthened by the same means that you chose to use.

SUZANNE But those means, madam, are open only to learned ladies.

MARCELINE And this poor child is all innocence—like an old judge!

BARTHOLO (*pulling* MARCELINE *away*) Goodbye, little bride of Figaro!

MARCELINE (*curtsying*) Also promised to the Count.

SUZANNE (*curtsying*) She gives you best regards, madam.

MARCELINE (*curtsying*) Will she also love me a little, madam?

SUZANNE (*curtsying*) As to that, pray have no fears.

MARCELINE (*curtsying*) Madam is as kind as she is pretty.

SUZANNE (*curtsying*) Enough, perhaps, to disconcert madam.

MARCELINE (*curtsying*) And above all, respectable.

SUZANNE (*curtsying*) That's a monopoly of dowagers.

MARCELINE (*outraged*) Dowagers, dowagers!

BARTHOLO (*interrupting her*) Marceline!

MARCELINE Let's go, doctor, or I shan't be able to restrain myself. Goodbye, madam. (*Curtsy*)

(*Exeunt*).

SUZANNE Go, madam; go, pedant. I am as little afraid of your plots as I am of your insults. Look at the old Sibyl! Because she has a little learning and used it to torment my lady in her youth, she wants to rule the castle. (*Throws the dress from her arm to a chair*) I've forgotten what I came for.

(*Enter* CHERUBINO).

CHERUBINO (*running in*) Suzy, I've been waiting two hours to catch you alone. I'm miserable: you're getting married and I'm going away.

SUZANNE   How does my getting married cause the departure of his lordship's favorite page?

CHERUBINO (*piteously*)   Suzanne: he's dismissed me!

SUZANNE (*mimicking him*)   Cherubino: what nonsense!

CHERUBINO   He found me yesterday at your cousin's, at Fanchette's. I was rehearsing her ingenue part in tonight's show and he flew into a rage on seeing me. "Get out," he said, "you little—" I don't dare repeat the bad word he used. "Get out! Tonight is your last night in this house!" If my lady, my dear godmother, doesn't calm him down about this, it's all over with me, Suzy; I'll never lay eyes on you again.

SUZANNE   On *me*? It's my turn, is it? So you don't go sighing around my lady any more?

CHERUBINO   Oh, Suzy. She is beautiful, majestic, but so—imposing!

SUZANNE   That is to say, *I* am not and you can take liberties.

CHERUBINO   You're mean! You know perfectly well I never dare take anything. How lucky you are, seeing her all the time, talking to her, dressing her in the morning, undressing her at night, unpinning each pin—oh, Suzy, I'd give anything—what's that in your hand?

SUZANNE (*mockingly*)   It's the blissful bonnet and the fortunate ribbon which enclose, at night, the hair of your beautiful godmother. . . .

CHERUBINO   Her ribbon—at night! Give it to me, be a dear, my love.

SUZANNE (*pulling it away*)   Not so fast. "His love!" What familiarity! If you weren't just a whippersnapper—(CHERUBINO *seizes the ribbon*) Oh, the ribbon!

CHERUBINO (*going behind and around the invalid chair*)   You can say you mislaid it, ruined it, lost it. Say anything you like.

SUZANNE (*chases after him around the chair*)   I promise you that in three or four years you will be the biggest little miscreant on earth! Give me back that ribbon. (*She snatches at it*)

CHERUBINO (*drawing a paper from his pocket*) Let me, do let me have it, Suzy. I'll give you my song here, and while the memory of my beautiful mistress will sadden all my days, the thought of you will bring me the only ray of joy that could lighten my heart.

SUZANNE (*tears the song out of his grasp*) "Lighten his heart!" the little scoundrel! Do you think you are talking to your Fanchette? My lord finds you with her; you breathe vows in secret to my lady; and on top of that you make me declarations to my face!

CHERUBINO (*excited*) It's true, on my honor! I don't know who I am or what I'm doing, but just lately, at the mere sight of a woman I've felt my breath come in gasps and my heart beat fast. The words "love" and "bliss" arouse and upset me. In short, the need to say to someone "I love you" has become so compelling that I say it to myself when I cross the park, I say it to our lady and to you, to the clouds and the wind that carries my useless words away. Yesterday I ran into Marceline—

SUZANNE (*laughing*) Ahahaha!

CHERUBINO Why not? She's a woman! She's a maid! A maid! A woman! Oh what sweet words are those—and how interesting!

SUZANNE He is losing his mind.

CHERUBINO Fanchette is very sweet: at least she listens to me and you don't.

SUZANNE What a pity! Let us listen to the gentleman. (*She snatches again at the ribbon*)

CHERUBINO (*turns and runs*) Not on your life! No one can take it, you see, except with *my* life. But if the price does not suit you, I'll increase it by a thousand kisses. (*He starts chasing her around the chair*)

SUZANNE (*turning on him as she flies*) A thousand slaps in the

face if you come near me. I'll complain to my lady, and far from
interceding for you I'll go to my lord and say: "Send back that
petty thief to his parents. He is a good-for-nothing who puts on
airs about being in love with Madam, and on the rebound tries to
kiss me."

CHERUBINO (*sees the Count entering and hides behind the armchair*)   That's the end of me!

SUZANNE   Coward! (*intercepts the Count and helps to conceal the
page*)

COUNT (*coming forward*)   You are upset, Suzette, you were talking to yourself. Your little heart seems to me full of agitation—
understandably enough on a day like this.

SUZANNE (*embarrassed*)   My lord, what do you want with me?
If someone saw us . . .

COUNT   I should hate to be surprised here. But you know the interest I take in you. Basil must have told you I love you. I have
only a moment to tell you so myself. Listen—(*he sits in the armchair*)

SUZANNE   I will not listen.

COUNT (*taking her hand*)   Just one word. You know the King
has made me ambassador to London. I am taking Figaro with me,
giving him an excellent post. Now since it is a wife's duty to follow her husband—

SUZANNE   Oh, if I had the courage to speak—

COUNT (*drawing her to him*)   Don't hesitate, speak, my dear.
Assume a privilege which you may use with me for life.

SUZANNE (*frightened*)   I don't want to, my lord, I don't want to.
Please leave me.

COUNT   But first tell me.

SUZANNE (*angrily*)   I don't know what I was saying.

COUNT   Something about a wife's duty.

SUZANNE   Very well. When you, my lord, eloped with your lady
from the doctor's house and married her for love, and when in her

honor you abolished that dreadful right of the lord of the manor—

COUNT   Which annoyed the girls so much, no doubt! Look, Suzette, it was a charming right and if you'll come and prattle with me about it this evening in the garden, I'll rate that little favor so high—

BASIL   (*speaking from without*)   He is not at home, my lord.

COUNT   (*rising*)   Whose voice is that?

SUZANNE   This is dreadful!

COUNT   Go out so that nobody comes in.

SUZANNE   (*upset*)   And leave you here?

BASIL   (*from outside*)   His lordship was with my lady, then he left; I'll go look for him.

COUNT   No spot where I can hide. Yes, behind that chair. It's not very good but—send him packing.

> (SUZANNE *bars his way; he gently pushes her; she retreats and thus comes between him and the page. But while the* COUNT *stoops and takes* CHERUBINO's *place, the latter throws himself kneeling on the seat and clings to the cushions.* SUZANNE *picks up the dress she formerly carried, drapes it over the page, and takes her stand in front of the chair*).

BASIL   (*entering*)   Did you by any chance see the Count, Miss?

SUZANNE   (*brusquely*)   How could I? Please go.

BASIL   (*coming nearer*)   If you only think a little you will see there was nothing surprising about my question. Figaro is looking for him.

SUZANNE   So he's looking for the man who is his worst enemy after yourself.

COUNT   (*aside*)   Let's see how he takes my part.

BASIL   Is it being a man's enemy to wish his wife well?

SUZANNE   Not in your book of rules, you vile corrupter.

BASIL   What does anyone ask of you that you aren't going to bestow on another? Thanks to a lovely ceremony, the things that were forbidden yesterday will be required tomorrow.

SUZANNE Disgusting wretch!

BASIL Marriage being the most comic of all serious things, I had thought—

SUZANNE (*outraged*) Contemptible thought! Who gave you leave to come in here!

BASIL There, there, naughty girl. God grant you peace! You'll do just as you like. But don't go thinking that I regard Mister Figaro as an impediment to my lord—and if it weren't for the little page . . .

SUZANNE (*shyly*) Don Cherubino?

BASIL (*mimicking her*) *Cherubino di amore,* yes. He's always buzzing about you and this morning again was at this door when I left you: say it isn't true.

SUZANNE What lies! Slanderer! Go away!

BASIL A slanderer because I see things as they are. Isn't it also for you the page has a song he carries mysteriously about him?

SUZANNE (*angrily*) For me indeed!

BASIL Unless he made it up for her ladyship. Truth to tell, when he serves at table, they say that he cannot take his eyes off her. But let him look out: my lord is a brute upon that point.

SUZANNE (*outraged*) And you are a scoundrel, going about spreading gossip and ruining a wretched child who is already in disgrace with his master.

BASIL Did I make it up? I say these things because everybody says them.

COUNT (*rising*) Who, everybody?

SUZANNE Heavens!

BASIL Ha ha!

COUNT Run along, Basil, and see that the boy is sent away.

BASIL I am truly sorry that I came in here.

SUZANNE (*upset*) Oh dear, oh dear!

COUNT She is faint, help her into the chair.

SUZANNE (*fending him off energetically*) I don't want to sit. To walk in here without leave is an outrage.

COUNT But there are two of us with you, my dear. There's not the slightest danger.

BASIL For my part, I deeply regret having made light of the page—since you overheard me. I was using it to ascertain her feelings, because essentially—

COUNT Fifty pounds, a horse, and back to his parents.

BASIL My lord, it was frivolous gossip.

COUNT A young libertine whom I found only yesterday with the gardener's daughter.

BASIL With Fanchette?

COUNT In her room.

SUZANNE (*outraged*) Where my lord had business also?

COUNT (*cheerfully*) That's an idea!

BASIL It is of good omen.

COUNT (*still cheerful*) Of course not. I was looking for your uncle Antonio, my drunken gardener, to give him some instructions. I knock. No one opens for quite a while. Your little cousin looks embarrassed. I grow suspicious while I talk to her and as I do so I cast an eye about. Behind the door there was a curtain of sorts, a wardrobe, something for old clothes. Without seeming to, I gently, slowly lift the curtain (*he illustrates by lifting the dress off the armchair*) and I see—(*he catches sight of* CHERUBINO)—I say!

BASIL Ha ha!

COUNT This is as good as before.

BASIL It's better.

COUNT (*to* SUZANNE) Congratulations, dear lady: hardly engaged to be married and yet able to manage such tricks! Was it to entertain my page that you wished to be alone? As for you, sir, whose behavior never varies, the only lack of respect for your godmother you had so far overlooked was to pay your addresses to her maid, who is the bride of your friend. But I will not allow Figaro, a man I love and esteem, to be the victim of this deception. Was he with you, Basil?

SUZANNE (*indignant*) There is no deception and no victim. (*pointing*) He was here while you were talking to me.

COUNT (*carried away*) I hope you lie when you say so. His worst enemy could wish him nothing worse.

SUZANNE He was asking me to beseech my lady to obtain his pardon from you. Your coming in upset him so much that he hid in the chair.

COUNT (*angrily*) Infernal cleverness! But I sat in that chair the moment I arrived.

CHERUBINO Alas, my lord, I was shaking in my shoes behind it.

COUNT Another trick! I stood there myself just now.

CHERUBINO Forgive me, but that is when I came around and crouched inside.

COUNT This young snake in the grass must be a—poisonous adder: he heard what we said?

CHERUBINO On the contrary, my lord, I did my best to hear nothing at all.

COUNT O treachery! (*To* SUZANNE) You shan't marry Figaro!

BASIL Moderation, if you please: someone's coming.

COUNT (*pulling* CHERUBINO *out of the armchair and setting him on his feet*). He would stay there in front of the whole world!

(*Enter* FIGARO, *the* COUNTESS, FANCHETTE, *with several footmen and country people dressed in white*).

FIGARO (*holding a woman's hat covered with white feathers and ribbons and speaking to the* COUNTESS) Only you, my lady, can obtain this favor for us.

COUNTESS You hear him, Count? They imagine that I wield an influence I do not in fact possess. Still, as their request is not unreasonable—

COUNT (*embarrassed*)   It would indeed have to be very much so—

FIGARO (*speaking low to* SUZANNE)   Back up my attempt—

SUZANNE (*the same to* FIGARO)   Which won't help any.

FIGARO (*in low voice*)   Never mind, do it.

COUNT (*to* FIGARO)   What is it you want?

FIGARO   My lord, your vassals, who are deeply touched by the abolition of a certain regrettable right that you gave up out of love for my lady—

COUNT   Well, the right *is* abolished; what are you getting at?

FIGARO   Only that it is high time the virtue of so good a master should be manifest. I myself stand to gain so much from it today that I want to be the first to glorify it at our wedding.

COUNT (*still more embarrassed*)   You can't be serious. The abolition of a shameful right is only the payment of a debt to decency. A Spaniard may want to conquer beauty by devotion, but to be the first to exact the sweetest of rewards as if it were a servile due— why, that's the tyrannical violence of a Vandal, not the acknowledged right of a Castilian nobleman!

FIGARO (*holding* SUZANNE's *hand*)   Then deign that this young creature, whose honor has been preserved by your noble reason, receive from your hand the virgin's coif of white feathers and ribbons as a symbol of the purity of your intentions. Have this ceremony become a custom at all weddings and let an appropriate chorus be sung each time to commemorate the event.

COUNT (*embarrassed*)   If I did not know that to be a lover, a poet, and a musician excused every kind of folly—

FIGARO   Join with me, my friends.

ALL (*together*)   My lord! my lord!

SUZANNE (*to the* COUNT)   Why brush aside an honor you so much deserve?

COUNT (*aside*)   Deceitful wench!

FIGARO   Look at her, my lord: no prettier face will ever signalize the extent of your sacrifice.

SUZANNE   Leave my face out of it and let us only praise his virtue.

COUNT   (*aside*)   The whole thing is a plot.

COUNTESS   I too join with them, Count, knowing as I do that this ceremony, ever to be cherished, owes its being to the gracious love you used to have for me.

COUNT   Which I still have, madam, and because of which I now yield.

ALL   (*together*)   Bravo!

COUNT   (*aside*)   I've been had. (*Aloud*) In order to give the ceremony yet more splendor, I should like to see it postponed till somewhat later. (*Aside*) Quick, let us get hold of Marceline!

FIGARO   (*to* CHERUBINO)   What about you, my lad, you don't applaud?

SUZANNE   He is in despair; his lordship is sending him home.

COUNTESS   Ah, my lord, I ask for his pardon.

COUNT   He doesn't deserve it.

COUNTESS   The poor boy is so young.

COUNT   Not so young as you think.

CHERUBINO   (*trembling*)   Clemency is not the lordly right you gave up when you married my lady.

COUNTESS   He only gave up the one that afflicted you all.

SUZANNE   If my lord had abandoned the right to pardon, it would surely be the first right he would want to restore in secret.

COUNT   (*embarrassed*)   Oh, quite.

COUNTESS   So what need to restore it?

CHERUBINO   (*to the* COUNT)   I was giddy in my actions, my lord, that is true. But there never was the least impropriety in my words.

COUNT   (*embarrassed*)   All right, that's enough.

FIGARO   What does he mean?

COUNT   (*sharply*)   Enough, enough! Everybody wants him pardoned: I so order it. I'll do more: I'll give him a company in my regiment.

ALL   (*together*)   Bravo!

COUNT But on one condition—that he leave at once to join up in Catalonia.

FIGARO Oh, my lord, make it tomorrow.

COUNT I have given an order.

CHERUBINO And I obey.

COUNT Salute your godmother and entreat her protection.

> (CHERUBINO *kneels on one knee before the* COUNTESS, *unable to utter a word*).

COUNTESS (*much moved*) Since you cannot stay even for today, young man, go. New duties call you: fulfill them worthily. Honor your benefactor. Remember this house where your youth was so leniently treated. Be upright, obedient, and brave. We shall all share in the pleasure of your success.

> (CHERUBINO *gets up and goes to where he stood before*).

COUNT You seem deeply moved, madam.

COUNTESS I do not apologize for it. Who knows what fate is in store for a child thrown into such a dangerous career? He is related to my family, as well as being my godson.

COUNT (*aside*) Basil was evidently right. (*Aloud*) Young man, give a kiss to Suzanne, for the last time.

FIGARO Why the last, my lord? He'll come and spend the winters with us. Give me a kiss too, captain. (*They embrace*) Goodbye, Cherubino. You are going to lead a very different life, my child. Thus: no more hanging about the women's quarters the livelong day, no more sweet drinks and pastries, no more blindman's buff and spinning the bottle. Just veteran soldiers, by God, weather-beaten and dressed in rags, a huge musket that weighs a ton— Right! turn! Left! turn! Forward! march! To glory—and don't you go stumbling on the way—unless a well-placed shot—

SUZANNE Horrors! be quiet!

COUNTESS What a send-off!

COUNT Where can Marceline be? Isn't it odd that she isn't with the rest of you?

FANCHETTE   My lord, she went walking to town, by the lane along the farm.

COUNT   And she is coming back?

BASIL   When it may please God.

FIGARO   May it please Him never to please . . .

FANCHETTE   The gentleman doctor was giving her his arm.

COUNT   (*quickly*)   The doctor is here?

BASIL   She fastened upon him at once . . .

COUNT   (*aside*)   He could not come at a better time.

FANCHETTE   She was all excited. She spoke very loud and paced back and forth and stopped and did like this with her arms. And the gentleman doctor, he did like this with his hand, to calm her down. She mentioned my cousin Figaro.

COUNT   (*taking her chin in his hand*)   Cousin . . . yet to be.

FANCHETTE   (*pointing to* CHERUBINO)   My lord, have you forgiven us for yesterday?

COUNT   (*interrupting*)   Good day, good day, my dear.

FIGARO   It's her confounded love that keeps her obsessed.* She would have spoiled our party.

COUNT   (*aside*)   She will spoil it yet, I promise you. (*Aloud*) Come, madam, let us go in. Basil, please stop in to see me.

SUZANNE   (*to* FIGARO)   You'll be joining me, sonny?

FIGARO   (*in low voice to* SUZANNE)   Wasn't he properly stuck?

SUZANNE   (*low*)   Delightful character!** (*Exeunt all but* FIGARO, CHERUBINO, *and* BASIL)

FIGARO   By the way, you fellows: the new ceremony having been adopted, the show tonight becomes a sequel to it. We mustn't forget our lines. Let's not be like those players who never act so poorly as on the night when the critics are wide awake. We haven't any tomorrow to recoup ourselves, so let's learn our parts today.

---

* This remark refers to Marceline, not to Fanchette.
** She means Figaro.

BASIL (*maliciously*) Mine is more difficult than you think.

FIGARO (*in pantomime, unseen by* BASIL, *pretends to give him a beating*) But you don't suspect the ovation you will get.

CHERUBINO Dear friend, you forget that I am leaving—

FIGARO —when you would like to stay.

CHERUBINO Oh, if I only could!

FIGARO Then, we must have a scheme. Not a murmur against your leaving. Traveling cloak on your shoulders. Make a show of packing, your horse at the gates, a brief gallop as far as the farm and come back on foot by the back way. My lord will think you gone: just keep out of his sight. I undertake to calm him down after the wedding party.

CHERUBINO But Fanchette does not know her role.

BASIL What the dickens were you teaching her this last week when you've hardly been away from her?

FIGARO You have nothing to do today—for heaven's sake coach her in her lines.

BASIL Be careful, young man, be careful! Her father is suspicious; the girl has been slapped and hasn't learned her lines—Cherubino, Cherubino, she will be sorry—the pot that goes once too often to the well . . .

FIGARO Ah, there's our curmudgeon with his old proverbs. Tell us, you old pedant, what the wisdom of nations has to say about the pot that goes to the well.

BASIL It gets filled.

FIGARO (*leaving*) Not so dumb as I thought.

ACT 2

A magnificent bedroom with a large bed in an alcove and a platform in front. The main door is upstage to the right, the dressing-room door downstage to the left. A third door, at the back, leads to the women's quarters. The window is on the opposite side.

SUZANNE *and the* COUNTESS *enter Right.*

COUNTESS (*throws herself into a wing chair*) Shut the door, Suzanne, and tell me everything in detail.

SUZANNE   I do not mean to hold back anything, my lady.

COUNTESS   And so he wanted to seduce you?

SUZANNE   Certainly not! My lord does not take that much trouble with servants: he wanted to buy me.

COUNTESS   And the little page was there all the while?

SUZANNE   Yes, that is to say he was hidden behind the big armchair. He had come to ask me to intercede with you for his pardon.

COUNTESS   Why not come to me direct? Do you suppose I would have refused him, Suzy?

SUZANNE   That's what I told him, but his sadness at leaving, especially at leaving you—"Ah, Suzy," he said, "how noble and beautiful she is, but how imposing!"

COUNTESS   Do I really look that way, Suzy, I who have always stood up for him?

SUZANNE   Then he saw the ribbon of your nightdress, which I had in my hand, and he jumped and grabbed it.

COUNTESS   (*smiling*)   My ribbon? What a child!

SUZANNE   I tried to take it from him, madam, but he was like a wild beast, his eyes shone: "You'll get it only with my life," he said, and his voice cracked.

COUNTESS   (*dreamily*)   And then, Suzy?

SUZANNE   Well madam, how can one put a stop to it? The little devil! "My godmother," he says, and "I wish I could," says he. And just because he wouldn't even dare kiss the hem of your gown, my lady, he always wants to be kissing me in earnest.

COUNTESS   (*still dreaming*)   Enough . . . enough nonsense. At last, then, my husband came to the point and told you . . .

SUZANNE   . . . that if I refused to listen to him, he would use his influence in behalf of Marceline.

COUNTESS   (*rising, pacing, and fanning herself vigorously*)   He does not love me at all any more.

SUZANNE   Why then is he so jealous?

COUNTESS   Like every husband, my dear—it is pride. Ah, I loved him too much. I wearied him with my caresses, bored him with my love. That is my chief wrong in relation to him. But I do not intend that his charming thoughts should bring you harm; you shall marry Figaro. He alone can help us: is he going to join us?

SUZANNE   As soon as the hunt is on its way.

COUNTESS   (*using her fan again*)   Open the window on the garden a bit. It's exceedingly warm in here.

SUZANNE That is because your ladyship has been talking and walking so actively. (*She opens the window at the back*)

COUNTESS (*absentmindedly*) In avoiding me of set purpose . . . men are creatures full of guilt.

SUZANNE (*shouting from the window*) There is my lord riding through the big field. Peter is with him and one, two, three, four—setters.

COUNTESS That gives us plenty of time. (*She sits*) Someone is knocking, Suzy.

SUZANNE (*runs singing to the door*) Why, it's my Figaro, it's my Figaro!

(*Enter* FIGARO).

SUZANNE Dear friend, come in. My lady can hardly wait.

FIGARO And what about you, little Sue? Her ladyship must not take on so. After all, what is all this fuss about?—a trifle. My lord Count finds our young lady charming and would like to make her his mistress—perfectly natural.

SUZANNE Natural?

FIGARO Then he appointed me king's messenger and my Suzy—er—attachée to the Embassy. No mental confusion there.

SUZANNE Are you through?

FIGARO And because Suzanne, my bride, declines the post and privileges, he wants to promote the plans of Marceline. Could anything be more simple? To seek revenge on those who thwart our purpose by interfering with theirs is what everybody does, it's what we ourselves are about to do. And that, so to speak, is that.

COUNTESS Figaro, how can you joke about a project that will rob us all of happiness?

FIGARO Who says it will, my lady?

SUZANNE Instead of sharing our grief, you—

FIGARO Isn't it enough that I am busy about it? No, no, let us be as methodical as he, and cool his desire for our belongings by arousing in him an apprehension for his own.

COUNTESS A good idea, but how?

FIGARO It is all done, madam. A piece of false information about you—

COUNTESS About me! You are out of your mind!

FIGARO No: it is he who must be driven out of his.

COUNTESS A man as jealous as he—

FIGARO So much the better. To make the most out of people like him, all you have to do is to whip up their blood—a device all women use. As soon as a man of his type is red hot with passion, the most trifling subterfuge enables one to lead him by the nose into the nearest fishpond. I have used Basil to deliver an anonymous note which informs his lordship that tonight a gallant will try to approach you during the ball.

COUNTESS You play fast and loose with the truth about a woman of honor?

FIGARO There are but few I would have dared to risk it with, madam, for fear of stating no more than the facts.

COUNTESS And now you'll expect me to thank you!

FIGARO Honestly, isn't it delightful to have cut out his work for him so that he will be prowling around his lady and swearing under his breath during the time that he counted on for dallying with mine? Already he is bewildered: will he gallop over this one, shall he mount guard over that one? (*At the window*) In his disturbed state of mind—look, look, how he races across the meadow after a poor hare who can't help himself! The hour of the wedding hastens on, but he won't be able to decide against it: he will never dare oppose it to my lady's face.

SUZANNE No, but Marceline, that *grande dame,* will not hesitate to dare.

FIGARO Ah! That doesn't worry me. Just let my lord know that you will meet him at dusk in the garden.

SUZANNE So that's your great device—to rely on him?

FIGARO See here: people who don't want to do anything about anything never achieve anything and aren't good for anything. That's my last word.

SUZANNE   A pleasant one!

COUNTESS   And so is her question: you really would let her meet him in the garden?

FIGARO   Not at all. I'll arrange for someone to put on one of Suzy's dresses. Taken in the act, how can he get out of it?

SUZANNE   Who will wear my dress?

FIGARO   Cherubino.

COUNTESS   He's gone.

FIGARO   Not as far as I'm concerned. Will the ladies allow me?

SUZANNE   One can always trust this fellow to hatch a scheme.

FIGARO   A scheme! Two, three or four at once, well scrambled and working from both ends against the middle: I was born to be a courtier.

SUZANNE   They say it's a difficult profession.

FIGARO   Accept, take, and ask—that's the secret in three words.

COUNTESS   He has so much self-confidence it rubs off on one!

FIGARO   That was my idea.

SUZANNE   You were saying?

FIGARO   That during the Count's absence I will send you Cherubino. Dress him up and do his hair and I'll conceal and indoctrinate him. After which, my lord, how you will dance! (*Exit*)

COUNTESS   (*holding her box of patches*)   Heavens, Suzy, I look a sight, and this young man is coming in!

SUZANNE   Don't you want him to get over it?

COUNTESS   (*gazing in the mirror*)   I? You'll see how I'm going to scold him!

SUZANNE   Let's get him to sing his romance. (*She lays it on the Countess's lap*)

COUNTESS   But really my hair is in a state—

SUZANNE   I'll just roll up these two curls; they will help your ladyship to scold him.

COUNTESS (*returning to reality*) What are you saying, Missy?

SUZANNE Come in, officer. We are visible.

(*Enter* CHERUBINO).

CHERUBINO (*trembling*) Oh how that title distresses me, madam. It tells me I must leave a place . . . a godmother . . . so good to me.

SUZANNE And so beautiful.

CHERUBINO (*with a sigh*) Oh, yes.

SUZANNE (*mimicking him*) "Oh, yes." The nice young man, with his long, hypocritical lashes. Come, bluebird, sing us a song for my lady.

COUNTESS (*unfolding the paper*) Whose is it?

SUZANNE See the guilty blush: it's a foot deep on his face.

CHERUBINO Is it forbidden to—cherish?

SUZANNE (*shaking her fist in his face*) I am going to tell on you, ne'er-do-well!

COUNTESS Enough. Does he sing?

CHERUBINO Please, madam, I am shaking all over.

SUZANNE (*laughing and mimicking*) Nya, nya, nya, nya, nya, nya, nya. As soon as madam wishes. These modest authors! I'll accompany him.

COUNTESS Take my guitar. (*Seated, she holds the paper to follow the words.* SUZANNE, *behind her armchair, begins the introduction, reading the notes over her mistress's head. The page stands in front, his eyes lowered. The scene duplicates the beautiful print made from Vanloo's painting entitled "Conversation in Spain."*)

(*To the tune of Malbrouck*)*

My weary steed astride

(Oh my heart, oh my heart, it is breaking)

* As in Beaumarchais, the verses do not everywhere fit the tune accurately. But his ballad being an early (though feeble) attempt to imitate folk poetry deserves to be translated as closely as possible.

Uncaring where, I ride
The solitary plain.

Uncaring where I ride,
No squire is at my side,
(Oh my heart, oh my heart, it is breaking)
For my godmother I pine,
And weep for her in vain.

For her I weep in vain,
And as the fates decree,
I carve upon a tree
(Oh my heart, oh my heart, it is breaking)
The letters of her name—
The king that moment came.

The king that moment came,
His bishops and his peers.
"Sweet page," spoke up the Queen,
(Oh my heart, oh my heart, it is breaking)
" 'Tis sore distress, I ween,
"That draws from you these tears.

"What draws from you these tears,
"Declare to us, poor lad."
"My lady Queen, my lord,
(Oh my heart, oh my heart, it is breaking)
"A godmother I had,
"Whom always I adored—

"Whom always I adored
"And I'll die dreaming of."
"Sweet page," the Queen implored,

(Oh my heart, oh my heart, it is breaking)
"That godmother you love,
"Pray let me take her place.

"Yes, let me take her place,
"And give you, page of mine,
"A maiden fair of face
(Oh my heart, oh my heart, it is breaking)
"A captain's daughter true,
"To whom I'll marry you."

"To whom I'll marry you!
"Those words I must deny,
"And for one favor sue:
(Oh my heart, oh my heart, it is breaking)
"To let me live in grief,
"And from my grieving die."

COUNTESS It is full of naïve simplicity, and even of true sentiment.

SUZANNE (*laying the guitar on a chair*) Oh, as far as sentiment goes, this young man is— But say, officer, have you been told that to enliven this evening's party we need to know whether one of my gowns will more or less fit you?

COUNTESS I'm afraid it won't.

SUZANNE (*comparing their statures*) He's about my size. Let's take off the coat. (*She takes it off him*)

COUNTESS What if someone comes in?

SUZANNE We're not doing anything wrong. I'll shut the door. (*She runs*) But it's the hair I want to see.

COUNTESS In my dressing room, a wrapper of mine.

(SUZANNE *goes into the dressing room*).

COUNTESS Until the ball opens, the Count will not know that you are still in the castle. We shall tell him afterwards that the time required to prepare your commission gave us the idea of—

CHERUBINO (*showing her the paper*) Unfortunately, madam, my commission is here, signed. Basil gave it to me from my lord.

COUNTESS Already! Not a minute lost. (*She reads*) In so much of a hurry that he forgot to affix the seal. (*She hands it back*)

SUZANNE (*carrying also a wide brimmed hat*) The seal to what?

COUNTESS His commission.

SUZANNE Already?

COUNTESS That's what I was saying. Is that the wrapper?

SUZANNE (*seated near the* COUNTESS) The handsomest of all. (*She sings with pins in her mouth*)

> Turn your head, oh Johnny my dear,
> Turn, my handsome cavalier.

(CHERUBINO *kneels beside her to have his hair dressed*).
Madam, he is sweet!

COUNTESS Pull his collar more like a woman.

SUZANNE There—look at that ragamuffin, what a pretty girl he makes. I'm jealous. (*She takes his chin in her hand*) Will you please not be so pretty as you are?

COUNTESS Silly girl! You must turn back the cuff so that the undersleeve shows up better. (*She lifts the sleeve*) What has he put on his arm?— a ribbon!

SUZANNE *Your* ribbon. I am glad madam saw it. I warned him I would tell on him. I swear, if my lord had not come in, I would have got the ribbon back. I'm almost as strong as he is.

COUNTESS I see blood. (*She takes off the ribbon*)

CHERUBINO (*shamefaced*) This morning, when I knew I had to leave, I was adjusting the snaffle on my horse. He tossed his head and the boss on the bit scratched my arm.

COUNTESS But why put a ribbon—

SUZANNE A *stolen* ribbon at that! Just imagine what the baffle— the snaffle—the raffle—I can't keep those things straight—look at that white skin! It's a woman's arm, whiter than mine, see? (*She compares*)

COUNTESS (*freezingly*)   Kindly get me some court plaster from my dressing table. (SUZANNE *gives* CHERUBINO *a shove, he falls forward on his hands. She goes into the dressing room. The* COUNTESS *remains silent a moment, her eyes on the ribbon.* CHERUBINO *gazes at her intently*) As to my ribbon, sir—it's the color I find most becoming to me—I was very much annoyed to be without it.

SUZANNE (*returning*)   The bandage for his arm. (*She gives the* COUNTESS *the plaster and a pair of scissors*)

COUNTESS   When you go for your dress, bring back the ribbon from some other bonnet. (SUZANNE *leaves by the center door, taking the page's coat with her*)

CHERUBINO (*eyes lowered*)   The ribbon you're taking from me would have cured me in no time.

COUNTESS   Owing to what specific virtue? (*Pointing to the plaster*) That is so much better.

CHERUBINO (*hesitating*)   When a ribbon . . . has bound the head . . . or touched the skin . . . of a person . . .

COUNTESS (*breaking in*)   . . . of a stranger, it cures wounds? That is news to me. I will test it by keeping the one you put around your arm. At the first scratch—on one of my maids—I shall try it out.

CHERUBINO (*deeply moved*)   You are keeping it—but I'm leaving!

COUNTESS   But not forever.

CHERUBINO   I'm so unhappy!

COUNTESS (*moved*)   Now he is weeping. It's Figaro's fault for prophesying—

CHERUBINO   Oh how I wish the time had come that he spoke about! If I were sure of dying at once, perhaps my lips would dare—

COUNTESS (*interrupts by wiping his eyes with her handkerchief*)

Be quiet, child, be quiet. There isn't a grain of sense in what you're saying. (*A knock at the door; she raises her voice*) Who is it?

COUNT (*outside*)   Why are you locked in?

COUNTESS (*upset*)   It's my husband. Heavens! . . . (*To* CHERUB-INO, *who has also got up*) You, without your coat, your collar open and your arms bare—alone with me—the general disarray —the anonymous letter he received, his jealousy—

COUNT (*outside*)   You won't open?

COUNTESS   The fact is . . . I am alone.

COUNT   Alone? With whom are you talking, then?

COUNTESS (*fumbling*)   With you, I should think.

CHERUBINO (*aside*)   After those scenes of yesterday and this morning he would kill me on the spot. (*He runs into the dressing room and shuts the door*).

COUNTESS (*removes the key and opens the other door to admit the* COUNT)   What a dreadful mistake!

COUNT (*somewhat severe*)   You are not in the habit of shutting yourself up.

COUNTESS (*upset*)   I was trying on—yes—odds and ends—with Suzanne. She went for a minute to her room.

COUNT   You look and sound quite strange.

COUNTESS   It's not surprising, not surprising at all, I assure you. We were speaking about you. She just left, as I said—

COUNT   You were speaking about me? Well, here I am. I've come back much disturbed. On setting out, I was handed a note— though I take no stock in it— it upset me.

COUNTESS   How so, what note, sir?

COUNT   You must admit, madam, that you or I must be sur-rounded by people who are—uncommonly wicked. Someone in-forms me that a person, whom I falsely suppose to be absent, will attempt to approach you.

COUNTESS   Whoever this rash being may be, he will have to make his way to this very spot, for I do not intend to stir for the rest of the day.

COUNT   What about tonight, for Suzanne's wedding?

COUNTESS   Not at any price; I am quite indisposed.

COUNT   Fortunately the doctor is here. (*The page overturns a chair in the dressing room*) What noise was that?

COUNTESS   (*distraught*)   Noise?

COUNT   Someone in there upset a piece of furniture.

COUNTESS   I—I heard nothing.

COUNT   You must be powerfully preoccupied.

COUNTESS   Preoccupied? What about?

COUNT   Madam: there is someone in that dressing room!

COUNTESS   Indeed, who could there be, sir?

COUNT   It is for me to ask that question: I have just arrived.

COUNTESS   It must be Suzanne putting things away.

COUNT   You told me she had gone to her room.

COUNTESS   Gone there—or here—I don't know which.

COUNT   If it is Suzanne, why your evident distress?

COUNTESS   Distress—over my maid?

COUNT   Over your maid it may be, but distress without a doubt.

COUNTESS   Without a doubt, sir, that girl concerns and occupies your mind much more than I.

COUNT   She concerns me so much that I want to see her at once.

COUNTESS   I readily believe that this is what you often want. But your ill-founded suspicions—

   (SUZANNE *enters at the back, unseen, with clothes in her arms*).

COUNT   If so, they will be easily dispelled. (*He speaks through the dressing-room door*) Come out, Suzanne, I order you to. (SUZANNE *stops near the alcove at the back*)

COUNTESS   She is almost naked, sir. How can you intrude in this way on women in their apartments? She was trying on some old things I am giving her on the occasion of her wedding. She fled when she heard you.

COUNT　If she is afraid to show herself, she can at least speak. (*He turns again to the closed door*) Answer me, Suzanne: are you in the dressing room? (SUZANNE, *still at the back of the alcove, hides behind the bed*)

COUNTESS (*quickly, to the closed door*)　Suzy, I forbid you to answer. (*To the* COUNT)　No one has ever carried tyranny so far!

COUNT (*turning again*)　If she won't speak, dressed or undressed I shall see her.

COUNTESS (*intercepting him*)　Anywhere else I can't prevent you, but I trust that in my own room—

COUNT　And I trust that in one minute I shall know who this mysterious Suzanne is. I can see it is useless to ask you for the key, but it is not hard to break down this trumpery door. Ho, there, anybody!

COUNTESS　You would bring in your people, create a public scandal—all on the strength of a vague suspicion!— We'll be the talk of the castle.

COUNT　An excellent point, madam, I can do without help. This instant I go to my rooms and return with what I need. (*He starts to go and turns back*) But in order that everything shall remain as it is, will you kindly accompany me, quietly and decently— since scandal displeases you so? My simple request will surely not be denied?

COUNTESS (*upset*)　Sir, who would dream of crossing you?

COUNT　Oh, I was forgetting: the door which leads to your maids' quarters. I must also shut it so that you may be fully vindicated. (*He shuts the center door and takes the key*)

COUNTESS (*aside*)　Oh what a fateful whim!

COUNT (*returning*)　Now that this chamber is sealed, I beg you to accept my arm. (*He raises his voice*) As for the Suzanne in the dressing room, she will have the goodness to await my return. The least of the evils that may befall her then is—

COUNTESS Really, sir, this is the most odious performance—

(*The* COUNT *leads her out and locks the door*).

SUZANNE (*runs from the alcove to the dressing-room door and speaks through the keyhole*) Open up, Cherubino, open, quick, it's Suzanne, open and hurry out.

CHERUBINO (*coming out*) Oh, Suzy, what a dreadful mess!

SUZANNE Go, go, you haven't a minute to lose.

CHERUBINO (*frightened*) How can I get out?

SUZANNE Don't ask me, just go.

CHERUBINO But I can't if I'm locked in.

SUZANNE After this afternoon's encounter he would break you, and she and I would be doomed. Go tell Figaro—

CHERUBINO Maybe the window over the garden isn't too high up. (*He runs to see*)

SUZANNE (*frightened*) A whole story—you can't do it! Oh my poor lady! And my marriage, dear God!

CHERUBINO (*coming back*) It overlooks the melon patch. All it would spoil is a couple of beds.

SUZANNE (*holding him back and crying out*) You will kill yourself!

CHERUBINO (*excited*) I'd throw myself into an open furnace—I would, Suzy—rather than cause her harm. And a kiss from you will bring me luck. (*Kisses her, runs toward the window, and leaps out*)

SUZANNE (*again cries out; then, overcome, falls into a chair; finally drags herself to the window and comes back*) He's off and away, the young devil! As light on his feet as he's pretty to look at. He'll have all the women he wants, I bet. Now to take his place, quick! (*Goes into the dressing room*) From here on, my lord, you can tear down the wall if it gives you pleasure, you don't get a word out of me. (*Shuts the door*)

(*The* COUNT *and* COUNTESS *return. He holds a pair of pliers which he soon throws upon a chair*).

COUNT Everything is as I left it. Madam, if you compel me to break down that door you must think of the consequences: once again, will you open it yourself?

COUNTESS But sir, what singular ill-temper can so destroy considerateness between husband and wife? If it were love that possessed you to the point of causing this fury, I could excuse it, however demented. The motive could make me forget the offense. But how can mere vanity move a well-bred man to such excesses?

COUNT Love or vanity, you open that door or I do it on the spot.

COUNTESS (*before the door*) My lord, please desist! Can you think me capable of forgetting what I owe to my self-respect?

COUNT Put it any way you like, madam, I mean to see who is in that dressing room.

COUNTESS (*frightened*) Very well, you shall see. But first listen to me quietly.

COUNT So it isn't Suzanne?

COUNTESS (*embarrassed*) At least it isn't a person . . . about whom you should have any . . . we were bent on a practical joke . . . quite harmless, really, for this evening . . . and I swear to you . . .

COUNT You swear to me—what?

COUNTESS That neither he nor I meant to offend you.

COUNT He—it is a man, then?

COUNTESS A child, dear sir.

COUNT And who, pray tell?

COUNTESS I hardly dare give his name.

COUNT (*furious*) I'll kill him!

COUNTESS Merciful powers!

COUNT Speak up!

COUNTESS The young . . . Cherubino.

COUNT That impudent whelp! That explains my suspicions—and the anonymous note.

COUNTESS (*her hands palm to palm in prayer*) Oh, sir, do not allow yourself to suppose—

COUNT (*stamping his foot and speaking aside*) That accursèd page turns up wherever I go. (*Aloud*) Come, madam, now that I know everything, open up. You would not have been so moved saying goodbye to him this morning, you would not have used such elaborate lies in your tale of Suzanne, and he would not have hidden so quickly and for so long, unless misconduct and guilt were the reason.

COUNTESS He was afraid of irritating you by showing himself.

COUNT (*beside himself, shouting at the dressing-room door*) Come out of there, you little scrub!

COUNTESS (*seizing the* COUNT *with both arms and thrusting him aside*) My dear sir, my dear sir, your anger makes me afraid for him. Don't, I beg, trust your own suspicions, which are unjust, and don't let his disheveled state—

COUNT Disheveled!

COUNTESS Alas, you will see—one of my bonnets on his head, without his coat, his neckband open and arms bare, ready to dress up as a woman. He was going to try to—

COUNT And you wanted to stay all day in your room! Worthless woman! You *shall* keep to your room—I'll see to it—and for a long time! But first I must kick out that insolent stripling that I may never come upon him again.

COUNTESS (*on her knees, arms uplifted*) Count, you must spare a mere child. I shall never forgive myself for being the cause of—

COUNT Your fears deepen his guilt.

COUNTESS He is not guilty—he was leaving. It is I who had him fetched.

COUNT (*in anger*) Get up. Remove yourself—shameless woman, to dare entreat me in behalf of another.

COUNTESS   Very well. I will remove myself, I will get up and give you the key to the door, but in the name of your love—

COUNT   My love, hypocrite!

COUNTESS   (*gets up and gives him the key*)   Promise that you will let the child go harmless—and may you vent your fury on me later if I do not convince you that—

COUNT   (*taking the key*)   I'm no longer listening.

COUNTESS   (*throws herself into an armchair, her handkerchief over her face*)   God, oh God, he will be killed!

COUNT   (*opens the door*)   You!

SUZANNE   (*comes out laughing*)   "I will kill him—I will kill him!" Why *don't* you kill him, your villainous page?

COUNT   (*aside*)   Lord! What a lesson! (*Looking at the* COUNTESS, *who is stupefied*)   And you pretend to be surprised, too? But perhaps Suzanne wasn't alone. (*He goes in*)

SUZANNE   (*going to* COUNTESS)   Recover yourself, madam, he's nowhere near—he jumped (*gesture*).

COUNTESS   Oh, Suzy, I am all in.

COUNT   (*emerges, vexed and silent*)   There's no one else and this time I was wrong. Madam, you are a good actress—

SUZANNE   What about me, my lord? (COUNTESS *holds her handkerchief to her mouth and says nothing, to regain her composure*)

COUNT   (*approaching*)   And so, madam, you were joking?

COUNTESS   (*recovering*)   And why not, sir?

COUNT   An absurd practical joke, and for what reason, tell me?

COUNTESS   Does your outrageous behavior deserve consideration?

COUNT   Do you call outrageous what relates to honor?

COUNTESS   (*gradually herself again*)   Did I join my life to yours only to be a perpetual victim of your neglect and your jealousy, two things which only you can reconcile?

COUNT   Ah, madam, you spare me nothing—

SUZANNE   She did! My lady had only to let you call the servants—

COUNT   You are right and I abase myself. Forgive me. I am discomfited.

SUZANNE   And deserve to be, you must admit.

COUNT   But why wouldn't you come out when I called to you?

SUZANNE   I was putting on some clothes as well as I could, with a multitude of pins: my lady's forbidding me to stir was for a good reason.

COUNT   Instead of reminding me of my error, help me to soothe her.

COUNTESS   No, my lord, an offense such as this is not to be palliated. I am about to retire to a convent. It is high time I did.

COUNT   Shall you be without regrets?

SUZANNE   For my part, I am sure the day you leave will be the beginning of endless grief.

COUNTESS   Even if it is, Suzy, I'd rather miss him than basely forgive him. He has wounded me too deeply.

COUNT   Rosine!

COUNTESS   I am Rosine no longer, the Rosine you so tenaciously pursued. I am the poor Countess Almaviva, the sad forsaken wife you no longer love.

SUZANNE   Oh, madam!

COUNT   (*suppliant*)   For charity's sake!

COUNTESS   When have you ever shown me any?

COUNT   But that anonymous letter—it curdled my blood.

COUNTESS   I did not agree to its being written.

COUNT   You knew about it?

COUNTESS   It was that harebrained Figaro—

COUNT   He was party to it?

COUNTESS   —who gave it to Basil—

COUNT   —who told me he had it from a peasant. Oh, sinister singing-master, two-faced underling: you shall pay for everybody's crimes!

COUNTESS How like a man! You beg for yourself a forgiveness you deny to others. Let me tell you: if ever I consent to pardon you for the error you committed on the strength of that note, I shall demand that the amnesty be general.

COUNT With all my heart, Countess. But how can I ever make up for so humiliating a blunder?

COUNTESS (*rising*) It humiliated us both.

COUNT No, no, only myself, believe me. But I am still amazed at the ease with which you women take on the proper look and tone of each circumstance. You were flushed, crying, your face was working—I assure you, you still look undone.

COUNTESS (*trying to smile*) I was flushing with resentment against your suspiciousness. But men are not delicate enough creatures to distinguish between the indignation of an honorable person suffering outrage and the confusion produced by a justified accusation.

COUNT (*smiling*) What about the disheveled page, coatless and half naked?

COUNTESS (*pointing to* SUZANNE) There he is. Aren't you glad to have caught this one instead of the other? Generally speaking, you do not hate to catch this one.

COUNT (*laughing*) And your entreaties and simulated tears?

COUNTESS You make me laugh and I do not feel like it.

COUNT We men think we are practiced in the art of politics, but we are children. It is you, you madam, whom the King should appoint ambassador to London! Your sex must have made a deep study of the art of controlling the countenance to succeed as you did today.

COUNTESS We are forced into it—and always by men.

SUZANNE But put us on parole and you will see what honorable beings we are.

COUNTESS Enough for the moment, Count. Possibly I went too far, but my leniency in so grave a case must be matched by yours.

COUNT   Do say again that you forgive me.

COUNTESS   Have I said it at all, Suzy?

SUZANNE   I did not hear it, madam.

COUNT   Well then, let the words slip out.

COUNTESS   You think you deserve it, you ungrateful man?

COUNT   I do, I do—because I repent.

SUZANNE   To suspect a man in my lady's dressing room!

COUNT   She has already punished me so severely!

SUZANNE   Not to believe her when she says it is her chambermaid!

COUNT   Rosine, are you unrelenting?

COUNTESS   Oh, Suzy, how weak I am! What a poor example I give you! (*Holding out her hand to the* COUNT) No one will ever believe again in a woman's anger.

SUZANNE   It's all right, madam. One always comes to this with men. (*The* COUNT *ardently kisses his wife's hand*)

FIGARO (*enters breathless*)   I heard that madam was seriously unwell. I've been running. I see there is no truth in the report.

COUNT (*drily*)   You are most attentive.

FIGARO   It is my duty. But since there is nothing in it, my lord, let me say that all your younger vassals of either sex are downstairs with their violins and pipes, awaiting the moment when you will allow me to bring my bride, so that they may accompany—

COUNT   And who will look after the Countess indoors?

FIGARO   Look after her—but she's not ill?

COUNT   No, but there is a mysterious stranger who will try to approach her.

FIGARO   What stranger?

COUNT   The man in the note that you gave to Basil.

FIGARO   Who said I gave him a note?

COUNT   Even if I hadn't been told, rascal, I could read it in your lying face.

FIGARO   Then it's my face deceiving you, not I.

SUZANNE Figaro, my poor darling, don't waste your eloquence in defeat: we told his lordship everything.

FIGARO Told what? You treat me as if I were Basil!

SUZANNE Told him you had written a note to make my lord believe that when he came in here he would find the young page in the dressing room where I shut myself up.

COUNT What have you to say to that?

COUNTESS There's no further need to conceal anything, Figaro, the joke is over.

FIGARO (*trying to guess*) The joke is over?

COUNT Yes, over, consummated: what do you say to that?

FIGARO Consummated? I say that—that I wish I could say the same about my marriage. You have only to give the word—

COUNT You admit the anonymous note?

FIGARO Since my lady wants it so, and Suzanne wants it so, and you want it so, I can't help wanting it too. But if I were you, my lord, really, I wouldn't believe a word of anything we are telling you.

COUNT You're always telling lies and always in the teeth of evidence; it's beginning to get on my nerves.

COUNTESS (*laughing*) The poor fellow! Why should you expect, sir, that he would tell the truth even once?

FIGARO (*low to* SUZANNE) I've warned him of the danger ahead —that's all a gentleman can do.

SUZANNE (*low*) Did you see the page?

FIGARO (*low*) Yes, all rumpled.

SUZANNE (*low*) Oh, wretched!

COUNTESS Look, my dear Count, they long to be united. Their impatience is understandable: let us go and celebrate the wedding.

COUNT (*aside*) But Marceline . . . where is Marceline? (*Aloud*) I'd like a moment to dress.

COUNTESS To be with our own people? You see what I have on.

ANTONIO (*enters half tipsy, holding a pot of partly crushed flowers*) My lord, my lord!

COUNT   What do you want with me, Antonio?

ANTONIO   I wish you'd have the windows over my beds fitted with bars. They throw every kind of thing out of those windows, a while back they threw out a man.

COUNT   Out of these windows?

ANTONIO   Just look at my gillyflowers!

SUZANNE (*low to* FIGARO)   Look out, Figaro, on your toes!

FIGARO   My lord, he gets drunk every day from the crack of dawn.

ANTONIO   You're wrong—with me there's always a little leftover from the day before. But that's how people judge you—in the dark.

COUNT (*breathing fire*)   The man, what man, where is he?

ANTONIO   Where he is?

COUNT   Yes, where?

ANTONIO   That's what *I* say. I want to have him found. I'm your servant. There's only me takes real care of your garden. Man falls on it—you can't help . . . appreciating . . . my reputation is . . . uprooted.

SUZANNE (*low to* FIGARO)   Change the subject, hurry!

FIGARO   Won't you ever give up drinking?

ANTONIO   If I didn't drink I'd go out of my mind.

COUNTESS   But to drink as you do, without thirst . . .

ANTONIO   To drink without thirst and make love at any time, my lady, 'swhat distinguishes us from the other animals.

COUNT (*fiercely*)   Answer me or I'll have you thrown on the parish.

ANTONIO   I wouldn't go.

COUNT   What's that?

ANTONIO (*touching his forehead*)   If *that* isn't enough to make you keep a good servant, on my side I'm not so dumb as to get rid of a good master.

COUNT (*shaking him violently*)　You say they threw a man out the window.

ANTONIO　Yes, excellency, just a while back, in a white vest, and he picked himself up and ran away.

COUNT (*impatient*)　And then?

ANTONIO　I tried to run after him, but I bumped into the fence so hard my finger (*he shows which*) is still numb. It can't move hand or foot of itself.

COUNT　But you'd recognize the man?

ANTONIO　That I could if I had seen him, as you might say.

SUZANNE (*low to* FIGARO)　He never saw him.

FIGARO　What a pother about a pot! How long do you mean to carry on about your bluebells, you old watering jug? No use asking, my lord, it was I who jumped down.

COUNT　You? Why?

ANTONIO　"How long I carry on," eh? Why, you must have grown since I saw you jump, 'cause you were smaller and thinner at the time.

FIGARO　Naturally: when one jumps one gathers oneself together.

ANTONIO　Methought 'twas rather the whippersnapper I saw—the page.

COUNT　Cherubino, you mean?

FIGARO　Of course, having come back—he and his horse—from the gates of Seville, where he probably is now.

ANTONIO　I didn't say that, I didn't say that! I didn't see a horse jump, or I'd say so.

COUNT　Oh to be patient!

FIGARO　I was in the women's quarters in my white vest—terribly hot day. I was waiting there for Suzanette, when suddenly I heard your voice, my lord, and a great noise going on. I don't know why, I was seized with fear—perhaps about the anonymous note. . . . To make a clean breast of it, I lost my head and jumped down on the flowers, spraining my ankle for my pains (*he rubs his foot*).

ANTONIO   As it's you, then I've got to give you back this bit of paper that fell out of your vest when you landed.

COUNT (*snatching it*)   Give it to me. (*He unfolds the paper and folds it again*)

FIGARO (*aside*)   This is the end.

COUNT (*to* FIGARO)   Your great fright has surely not made you forget the contents of this paper, nor how it got into your pocket?

FIGARO (*embarrassed, looks into all his pockets, bringing out letters and papers*)   Oh certainly not—but I carry so many about me —every one has to be answered. (*He looks at a paper*) This, for instance, what's—? ah, yes, a letter from Marceline, four pages, a beautiful letter. Could that other one be the petition from that poacher who is in prison? No—here it is. I also had a list of the furniture in the pavilion, in my other pocket—(*The* COUNT *reopens the paper in his hand*)

COUNTESS (*low to* SUZANNE)   Heavens, Suzy, it's the officer's commission.

SUZANNE (*low to* FIGARO)   We're undone: it's the commission!

COUNT (*folding the paper*)   Well, resourceful sir, you can't guess?

ANTONIO (*going toward* FIGARO)   My lord says as how can't you guess?

FIGARO (*pushing him away*)   Hence, varlet, and don't speak into my nose!

COUNT   You cannot recall for me what the paper might be?

FIGARO   Ah, ah, ah! I have it!—the poor boy! It must be Cherubino's commission, which the dear child showed me and I forgot to give back. What a scatterbrain I am! But how can he manage without his commission? We must go after him—

COUNT   Why should he have given it to you?

FIGARO (*embarrassed*)   He wanted—something done to it.

COUNT (*looks at paper*)   There's nothing needs doing.

COUNTESS (*low to* SUZANNE)   The seal.

SUZANNE (*low to* FIGARO) The seal's not on it.

COUNT (*to* FIGARO) You have nothing to say?

FIGARO Yes, the fact is . . . something *is* missing. He says it is customary.

COUNT Customary? What is customary?

FIGARO To affix the seal showing your coat of arms. But perhaps it isn't worth the trouble.

COUNT (*reopens the paper and crumples it up angrily*) Confound it! My fate decrees that I'm to be kept in the dark. (*Aside*) This—this Figaro is the master mind, and I—I should keep from striking back! (*He starts to stalk out*)

FIGARO (*stopping him*) You're not going without giving the word about my wedding?

(*Enter* BASIL, BARTHOLO, MARCELINE, *and* SUNSTRUCK).

MARCELINE (*to the* COUNT) Don't give the word, my lord. Before you do him a favor, you must do me justice. He has obligations toward me.

COUNT (*aside*) My revenge at last!

FIGARO Obligations? Of what sort? Please explain.

MARCELINE Of course I shall explain, false knave! (COUNTESS *sits in an armchair,* SUZANNE *behind her*)

COUNT What is it you are referring to, Marceline?

MARCELINE A promise of marriage.

FIGARO A promissory note for money I borrowed, nothing more.

MARCELINE (*to* COUNT) But with the forfeit of marrying me. You are a great lord, the highest judge in the province . . .

COUNT Come to the assizes. I will give everybody justice.

BASIL (*pointing to* MARCELINE) In that case, Your Worship will permit me to put in evidence my claims on Marceline?

COUNT (*aside*) This is the scoundrel of the anonymous note.

FIGARO As mad as she is—birds of a feather!

COUNT (*to* BASIL, *angrily*) Your claims, your claims! What right have you to speak up in my presence, master fool?

ANTONIO (*striking his fist into the palm of his other hand*)   Got it the first time: it sure is his right name!

COUNT   Marceline, everything is recessed until the public hearing of your plea, which shall take place in the large reception room. You, wise Basil, as my faithful and reliable agent, shall go into town and summon the bench.

BASIL   For her case?

COUNT   And bring along the peasant who gave you the note.

BASIL   How shall I know him?

COUNT   You object?

BASIL   I did not enter your service to run errands.

COUNT   What's that?

BASIL   A talented performer on the parish organ, I teach my lady the keyboard, coach her women in singing and your pages on the mandolin. But my chief employment is to entertain your company on the guitar, when it pleases you to command me.

SUNSTRUCK (*coming forward*)   I'll go, your lordsy, if they's what you want.

COUNT   What is your name and your employment?

SUNSTRUCK   My name is Sunstruck, good lordsy. I watch the goats, and bin asked in for the fireworks. It's holiday today for all us herds. But I know where's the roaring big trial-shop in town.

COUNT   Your gumption pleases me, go do my errand. As for you, (*to* BASIL) go along with the gentleman, singing and playing the guitar to entertain him on the way, for he is of my company.

SUNSTRUCK (*elated*)   I—I'm of the—(SUZANNE *calms him down by pointing to the* COUNTESS)

BASIL (*taken aback*)   Go along with Sunstruck while playing the guitar?

COUNT   It is your profession: off you go, you're dismissed. (*Exit*)

BASIL (*to himself*)   I'm certainly not going to fight the iron pot, I who am—

FIGARO   —already cracked.

BASIL   (*aside*) Instead of furthering their wedding, I am going
to insure Marceline's and mine. (*To* FIGARO) Don't sign anything,
I warn you, until I come back. (*He picks up his guitar from a*
chair at the back)

FIGARO   (*following him*) Sign anything? Don't worry! I shan't,
even if you never come back. But you don't seem in the mood for
song. Would you like me to begin? Come on, a smile, and the
high *la-mi-la* for my bride. (*He walks backward and dances the*
following Seguidilla. BASIL *accompanies him and everyone joins*
in).

> Better than riches, I love
>   The goodness of
>   My Suzanne,
> Zann, zann, zann,
> Zann, zann, zann,
> Zann, zann, zann
>
> Always on her I'll depend
>   And madly end
>   As I began
> Gan, gan, gan,
> Gan, gan, gan,
> Gan, gan, gan.
> (*Exeunt singing and dancing*).

COUNTESS (*in the wing chair*) You see, Suzanne, the ordeal I
had to go through, thanks to your wild friend's anonymous note?

SUZANNE   Oh, madam, if you could have seen your face when I
came out of the dressing room—you lost all your color, but only
for an instant, then you grew red—oh so red!

COUNTESS And he jumped out of the window?

SUZANNE Without a moment's hesitation, the dear child—light as a bird.

COUNTESS That deplorable gardener! The whole thing made me so dizzy I couldn't keep two ideas together in my mind.

SUZANNE Not at all, my lady, on the contrary. I saw at once what facility the habit of high society confers on respectable ladies who have to tell lies.

COUNTESS Do you think the Count was taken in? What if he finds the poor child in the castle?

SUZANNE I'm going to make sure he is well hidden.

COUNTESS He must go away. After what happened, you can imagine I'm not tempted to send him into the garden dressed like you.

SUZANNE And I shan't go either, so once again my wedding is—

COUNTESS Wait! What if in your place, or another's—why shouldn't I go?

SUZANNE You, madam?

COUNTESS No one could be reprimanded—and the Count couldn't explain the facts away. First to have punished jealousy, and then to demonstrate his infidelity—it would be . . . ! Come, our luck in the first adventure encourages me to try a second. Let him know quickly that you will go into the garden. But be sure no one knows—

SUZANNE Not Figaro?

COUNTESS No, no. He would want to contribute ideas . . . Fetch me my stick and my velvet mask. I'll go out on the terrace and daydream. (SUZANNE *goes into the dressing room*)

COUNTESS My scheme is surely brash enough. (*turns around*) Ah, my ribbon, my pretty ribbon, I had forgotten you. (*She takes it, sits, and rolls it up*) Henceforth you will be with me always, you will remind me of the scene in which that poor boy . . . Oh,

Count, what have you done!—and what am *I* doing right now? (SUZANNE *re-enters; the* COUNTESS *furtively slips the ribbon into her bosom*)

SUZANNE   Here is the stick and your mask.

COUNTESS   Remember, I forbid you to say one word to Figaro.

SUZANNE (*joyful*)   Your plan is delightful, my lady. I've been thinking about it. It brings everything together, concludes everything, embraces everything. Whatever comes of it, my marriage is now assured. (*She kisses the Countess's hand. Exeunt*)

During the intermission, the courtroom is prepared. Two settees are brought in for counsel, one on each side of the stage, but allowing free passage behind. In the center, toward the back, a raised platform with two steps, on which is put the Count's chair of state. The clerk's table and his stool are to one side downstage; seats for Bridlegoose and the other judges are placed alongside the Count's platform.

ACT 3

*A room in the castle, known as the throne room and used as
a reception room. To one side a canopy over a monumental
chair, and on the wall, a portrait of the King. The* COUNT
with PETER, *who is wearing coat and boots and is holding a
sealed package.*

COUNT (*speaking fast*)   It's clearly understood?
PETER   Yes, your Excellency. (*Exit*)
COUNT (*shouting*)   Peter!
PETER (*returning*)   Excellency?
COUNT   No one saw you?
PETER   Not a soul.
COUNT   Take the arab.
PETER   He's at the garden gate saddled and ready.
COUNT   Straight to Seville without a stop.
PETER   It's only ten miles and a fair road.

COUNT   As soon as you arrive, find out if the page is there.

PETER   At the house?

COUNT   Yes, and how long he's been there.

PETER   I understand.

COUNT   Give him his commission and come back as fast as you can.

PETER   What if he isn't there?

COUNT   Come back even faster. Tell me at once. Quick, be off!
  (*Exit* PETER).

COUNT (*pacing and meditating*)   It was clumsy of me to send Basil away . . . Anger is a bad counselor. . . . That note he gave me telling of an attempt to approach the Countess . . . The chambermaid locked in that room when I come back . . . Her mistress making believe she was a prey to terror, or really terrified. . . . A man jumps out of the window and the other, later, owns up to it, or pretends it was he. There is a link missing. Something devious is going on. A certain license among my vassals—what can it matter? But the Countess, if some upstart dared! . . . my mind wanders. Truly, when anger rules, the most controlled imagination runs wild, as in a dream. She was laughing—I heard her smothered giggles, their ill-concealed amusement. But she has self-respect . . . and my honor—in whose keeping is it? As to the other affair, where do I stand? Did that rascally Suzanne give me away?—seeing it isn't *her* secret yet. Why am I so bent on having her? A dozen times, I've thought of giving her up. The results of indecision are certainly strange: if I wanted her without hesitation, I shouldn't feel nearly so much desire. Figaro is behind time as usual: I must deftly plumb his thoughts. (FIGARO *enters upstage and stops*) At any rate I must find out from his replies to what I shall put to him casually whether or not he knows I'm in love with Suzanne.

FIGARO (*aside*)   Here it comes.

COUNT   That is, if she has dropped a hint.

FIGARO (*aside*) I guessed it, I guess.

COUNT Next, I marry him off to the old girl . . .

FIGARO (*aside*) Mister Basil's belovèd?

COUNT And then see what I can do with the young one.

FIGARO (*aside*) With my wife, if you please.

COUNT (*turning around*) Eh, what? Who is it?

FIGARO Me, at your service.

COUNT What were you saying?

FIGARO I haven't breathed a word.

COUNT "My wife, if you please."

FIGARO Oh that!—That is the conclusion of a reply I was making: "Go and tell my wife, if you please."

COUNT (*pacing*) His wife! I am curious to know what business can detain your lordship when I have you called.

FIGARO (*pretending to adjust his clothing*) I'd got dirty falling on that flowerbed, so I changed.

COUNT Does it take an hour?

FIGARO It takes the time it takes.

COUNT The servants here need longer to dress than the masters.

FIGARO That's because they have no valets to help them.

COUNT I didn't quite understand what compelled you a moment ago to risk your life for nothing by jumping—

FIGARO Risk my life! One would suppose I had leaped into a bottomless pit!

COUNT Don't try to put me off the point by pretending you missed it yourself, you devious lackey. You understand very well that it isn't the danger to your life that concerns me, but your motive.

FIGARO On the strength of a false alarm you come rushing in furiously, overturning everything like a mountain torrent. You're looking for a man: you have to find one or you will break down the doors and splinter the walls! I happen to be in your way—how am I to know that in your wrath—

COUNT   You could have escaped by the stairs—

FIGARO   And you'd catch me in the hall.

COUNT (*angry*)   In the hall! (*Aside*) I'm getting the worst of it, and no nearer finding out what I am after.

FIGARO (*aside*)   Let us see his game and match him trick for trick.

COUNT (*softening his tone*)   That isn't what I wanted to tell you. Let's drop the subject. I thought—as a matter of fact, I did think of taking you with me to London, as King's Messenger, but on second thoughts—

FIGARO   Your lordship has changed his mind?

COUNT   In the first place you don't know English.

FIGARO   I know "God damn!"

COUNT   I don't follow you.

FIGARO   I say that I know "God damn!"

COUNT   What about it?

FIGARO   I mean, English is a wonderful language—it takes but a few words to cover a lot of ground. With "God damn," in English, a man need lack for nothing. Do you want to sink your teeth into a nice juicy fowl? Go into a tavern and make this gesture (*turning a spit*) and say "God damn!" The waiter brings you a joint of salt beef with no bread—it's marvelous! Do you want a good glass of burgundy or claret—just do this (*drawing a cork*) "God damn!" and they bring you a foaming tankard of beer—it's perfectly wonderful! Should you meet one of those attractive ladies who go trotting about with their elbows pulled back and their hips swinging a bit, just put your four fingers delicately on your lips—"God damn!"—and you get slapped as by a stevedore. That proves they get your meaning. The English people, it is true, use a word or two more, here and there in conversation, but it is clear that "God damn" is the core of the language—so if your only reason for leaving me behind in Spain is—

COUNT (*aside*)   He wants to go to London: she hasn't told him.

FIGARO (*aside*)   He thinks I know nothing. Let's encourage his delusion.

COUNT   What motive did the Countess have for playing that trick on me?

FIGARO   Really, my lord, you know the reason better than I.

COUNT   I anticipate all her wishes and smother her with gifts.

FIGARO   You give but you aren't faithful: would anyone be grateful for luxuries who is starved of necessities?

COUNT   You used to tell me everything.

FIGARO   And now I keep nothing from you.

COUNT   How much did the Countess give you for being in league with her?

FIGARO   How much did you give me to extricate her from Bartholo's hands?* Look here, my lord, it's best not to humiliate a man who serves you well, for fear he may turn into a nasty underling.

COUNT   Why is there something shady about everything you do?

FIGARO   Things always look bad when someone's bent on finding fault.

COUNT   You have a hateful reputation!

FIGARO   Maybe it's undeserved: how many noblemen can say as much?

COUNT   Time and again I've seen you on the path to fame and fortune—you always go astray.

FIGARO   What do you expect? The mob is all around, pushing, struggling, crowding, using their elbows, knocking you down. Survives who can; the rest are crushed. And so my mind's made up: I'm through.

COUNT   Through with success? (*Aside*) That's news.

FIGARO (*aside*)   My turn now. (*Aloud*) Your excellency favored me with the stewardship of the castle: my lot is a happy one. True,

---

* The implied answer is: "Nothing." The allusion is to the plot for freeing Rosine in *The Barber of Seville*.

I shan't be King's Messenger and be the first to hear interesting news; but by way of compensation, I'll enjoy wedded bliss here in the heart of Andalusia.

COUNT Why not take your wife to London?

FIGARO I'd have to leave her so often I'd soon find marriage a bore.

COUNT With your brains and character, you could make your way in the administration.

FIGARO Make your way with brains? You must think mine are addled: be dull and obsequious if you want to succeed.

COUNT All you'd have to do is to learn statecraft under me.

FIGARO I know all about it.

COUNT As you do English—the basic tongue?

FIGARO Yes—and it's nothing to boast about. Only pretend not to know what you do know and vice versa; understand what's unintelligible and fail to take in what is clear; above all, put forth more strength than you possess; make a secret, often, of what no one is hiding; shut yourself up and trim goosequills so as to seem deep when you are only, as they say, a stuffed shirt; play a part well or ill, send out spies and hire informers, tamper with seals and intercept letters, and try to make ignoble tricks look noble in the light of important ends—that's all of statecraft or God strike me dead!

COUNT But that's mere intrigue you're describing.

FIGARO Statecraft, intrigue—as you like. To me, they're kith and kin, and the world is welcome to them. "I'd rather have my own best girl" as the man told the king in the ballad.*

COUNT (*aside*) He wants to stay. I see . . . : Suzanne gave me away.

FIGARO (*aside*) I've scored and paid him back in his own coin.

COUNT And so you hope to win your case against Marceline?

---

* *J'aime mieux ma mie, o gué*, a song of the time of Henry IV which is quoted in Molière's *Misanthrope*.

FIGARO   Do you impute it to me as a crime that I refuse an old maid when Your Excellency feels free to snatch all the young ones?

COUNT (*bantering*)   On the bench the judge will put self aside and heed nothing but the law.

FIGARO   The law!—lenient to the great, harsh to the humble.

COUNT   Do you think I am joking?

FIGARO   Who knows, my lord? But *Tempo è galant'uomo,* as the Italian proverb says. Time always tells the truth—that's how I'll learn what good or ill is to befall me.

COUNT (*aside*)   I can see she's told him everything; he's got to marry the duenna.

FIGARO (*aside*)   He thinks he has me fooled. Actually, what has he found out?

(*Enter* FOOTMAN).

FOOTMAN (*announcing*)   Don Guzman Bridlegoose.*

COUNT   Bridlegoose?

FIGARO   Of course! the associate justice, your understudy and right-hand man.

COUNT   Let him wait. (*Exit* FOOTMAN)

FIGARO (*waiting a moment longer while the* COUNT *is abstracted*) What else did your lordship require?

COUNT (*wide awake*)   I? I was saying this room should be prepared for the public hearing.

FIGARO   It's all set: the big chair for you, pretty good chairs for the justices, the clerk's stool, benches for the lawyers, the foreground for the quality and the rest of the floor for the groundlings. I shall dismiss the cleaning women. (*Exit*)

COUNT (*to himself*)   That upstart is becoming a nuisance. When he argues he gets the best of me. He presses in and corners you.

---

* The don's first name is an allusion to the judge whom Beaumarchais fought and satirized in the course of a protracted lawsuit. Bridlegoose is from Rabelais, though Beaumarchais modestly changed the name to "Bridlegosling" to suggest his descent.

Oh fox and vixen! You have combined to take me in. Well, be friends, be lovers, be what you will—I don't care. But when it comes to marrying—

    (*Enter* SUZANNE).

SUZANNE (*breathless*)   My lord, forgive me, my lord.

COUNT (*crossly*)   What is it, miss?

SUZANNE   You are angry?

COUNT   I take it there is something you want?

SUZANNE (*shyly*)   It's because my lady has the vapors. I ran to ask you to lend us your bottle of ether. I'll bring it back immediately.

COUNT (*giving it to her*)   Never mind. Keep it for yourself: you'll soon need it.

SUZANNE   Do women of my sort have vapors too? Isn't it a class disease, which is caught only in boudoirs?

COUNT   Well, a girl who is in love and engaged and who loses her intended—

SUZANNE   But if he pays Marceline out of the dowry you promised me—

COUNT   *I* promised you?

SUZANNE (*lowering her eyes*)   Sir, I believe I heard you say so.

COUNT   You did, but only if on your side you were willing to listen to me.

SUZANNE (*eyes still lowered*)   Isn't it my duty to listen to you?

COUNT   Then, cruel girl, why didn't you tell me sooner?

SUZANNE   It's never too late to tell the truth.

COUNT   You'll come into the garden tonight?

SUZANNE   As if I didn't go walking there every evening.

COUNT   This morning you behaved very harshly to me.

SUZANNE   This morning, yes, with the page behind the armchair.

COUNT   You are right. I forgot. But why your stubbornness before, when Basil spoke to you on my behalf?

SUZANNE   Why should someone like Basil—

COUNT You are *always* right. Still, there is a certain Figaro to whom I think you have told everything.

SUZANNE To be sure: I tell him everything . . . except what need never be told.

COUNT (*laughing*) You darling! You promise, then? If you break your word—let's be clear about it, sweetheart—no dowry, no marriage.

SUZANNE (*curtsying*) By the same token, my lord, no marriage, no right of the lord of the manor.

COUNT Where does she learn this repartee? I swear, I'm crazy about her—but your mistress is waiting for the ether.

SUZANNE (*laughing and giving back the bottle*) How could I have talked to you without a pretext?

COUNT (*trying to kiss her*) Lovely creature!

SUZANNE (*running off*) People are coming.

COUNT (*aside*) She is mine! (*He runs off*)

SUZANNE Quick, now, to report to my lady.

FIGARO (*enters*) Suzanne, Suzanne, where are you off to in such a hurry after leaving my lord?

SUZANNE You can go to court now, you've just won your suit. (*Running offstage*)

FIGARO (*following*) See here—(*Exit*)

COUNT (*returning*) "You've just won your suit"! So I was pitching headlong into a trap! O my dear damnable schemers, you will rue the day! . . . a sound, solid decision from the bench . . . of course, he might pay off the duenna . . . but what with? If he should pay. . . . Ah, ah, I have the proud Antonio, whose worthy ambition looks down on Figaro as rootless and unworthy of his niece. By nursing this idée fixe—and why not? In the field of intrigue one must cultivate everything, even the vanity of fools. (*He starts to call*) Anto- —(*sees* MARCELINE *and others, exit*)

(*Enter* MARCELINE, BARTHOLO, *and* BRIDLEGOOSE).

MARCELINE *to* BRIDLEGOOSE Sir, pray listen to my case.

BRIDLEGOOSE (*gowned and stammering slightly*) Very well, let us s-s-speak of it verbally.

BARTHOLO It's a promise of marriage—

MARCELINE Linked with a loan of money.

BRIDLEGOOSE I und-derstand, etcetera and the rest.

MARCELINE No sir, no etcetera.

BRIDLEGOOSE I und-derstand: you have the money?

MARCELINE No sir, it was I who lent it.

BRIDLEGOOSE I quite und-derstand: you want the money back.

MARCELINE No sir, I want him to marry me.

BRIDLEGOOSE I told you I und-derstood. But he—does he want to m-marry you?

MARCELINE No sir, that is the point of the case.

BRIDLEGOOSE Do you mean to imply that I do not und-derstand the case?

MARCELINE No sir, (*to* BARTHOLO) What a spot we're in! (*To* BRIDLEGOOSE) You say you are going to decide the case?

BRIDLEGOOSE Why else would I have bought my j-judgeship?

MARCELINE (*sighing*) It seems to me a great wrong to sell them.

BRIDLEGOOSE True, it would be better to g-give them to us for n-nothing. Whom are you suing?

(*Enter* FIGARO *rubbing his hands*).

MARCELINE (*pointing*) That unscrupulous man!

FIGARO (*cheerfully to* MARCELINE) Perhaps I'm in your way? My lord will be back in a moment, Your Worship.

BRIDLEGOOSE I've seen that fellow somewhere.

FIGARO In the house of your lady wife, at Seville, and in her service, counselor.

BRIDLEGOOSE In what year?

FIGARO A little less than a year before the birth of your younger son, who is a very pretty child if I do say so myself.

BRIDLEGOOSE Yes, he is the b-best-looking of them all. They tell me here that you are up to your old tricks. ·

FIGARO   You flatter me, sir. It's only a trifle.

BRIDLEGOOSE   A promise of marriage! What a booby it is!

FIGARO   Sir!

BRIDLEGOOSE   Have you seen my secretary, a very nice chap?

FIGARO   You mean Doublefist, the clerk?

BRIDLEGOOSE   Yes, I do. He feeds in two places, too.

FIGARO   Feeds! I'll swear he wolfs. Yes indeed, I saw him about the writ, and then again about the supplement to the writ, as is customary.

BRIDLEGOOSE   Forms must be observed.

FIGARO   Unquestionably. Just as the cause of the suit belongs to the parties, so the forms are the property of the court.

BRIDLEGOOSE   The lad is not so stupid as I thought at first. Well, friend, since you know so much, we'll t-take care of you in court.

FIGARO   Sir, I rely on your sense of equity even though you are one of our justices.

BRIDLEGOOSE   What? . . . It's true I am a j-justice. But what if you owe and don't pay?

FIGARO   Surely you can see it comes out exactly as if I didn't owe.

BRIDLEGOOSE   No d-doubt . . . what? What? What did he say?
     (*Enter the* COUNT *and a beadle, who walks ahead of him shouting for silence*).

COUNT   Gown and bands in this place, Master Bridlegoose? For a hearing in camera, ordinary clothes are good enough.

BRIDLEGOOSE   'Tis you are good enough, my lord. But I never go out ung-gowned, don't you see, it is a matter of f-form. A man will laugh at a judge in a short coat but tremble at the sight of an attorney in a g-gown, thanks to the f-form, the f-form.

COUNT   Let the court convene.

BEADLE   (*Croaking as he opens the doors*)   The court! The court!
     (*Enter* ANTONIO, *the Count's servants and his tenants, men and women, who are dressed for the wedding. The* COUNT *sits in the big chair,* BRIDLEGOOSE *to one side, the clerk on*

his stool. The justices and counsel on the benches, MAR-
CELINE *next to* BARTHOLO, FIGARO *on another bench, the servants and tenants behind them*).

BRIDLEGOOSE (*to the clerk*) Doublefist, call up the cases.

DOUBLEFIST (*reading from a paper*) The noble, high, and puis-
sant Don Pedro George, Hidalgo and Baron de los Altos y Montes
Fieros y otros montes *v.* Alonzo Calderón, a young playwright, in
the matter of a stillborn play, which each disowns and attributes to
the other.

COUNT They are both right. With a view to insuring public attention if they write another work together, it is ordered that the
nobleman shall contribute his name and the poet his talent. Case
dismissed.

DOUBLEFIST (*from another paper*) Andrea Petrucchio, farmer, *v.*
the tax collector, in the matter of an arbitrary foreclosure.

COUNT Not within my jurisdiction. I shall serve my vassals best
by sponsoring them at the King's court. Next.

DOUBLEFIST (*reading a third paper.* BARTHOLO *and* FIGARO *rise*)
Barbara Hagar Rahab Magdeleine Nicola Marceline Greenleaf
spinster of age (MARCELINE *rises and bows*) *v.* Figaro, first name
missing—

FIGARO Anonymous.

BRIDLEGOOSE Anonymous? What patron s-saint is that?

FIGARO Mine.

DOUBLEFIST (*writing*) "*versus*—Anonymous Figaro." Profession?

FIGARO Gentleman.

COUNT You a gentleman? (*The clerk is still writing*)

FIGARO God willing, I should have been the son of a prince.

COUNT (*to the clerk*) Go on.

BEADLE (*croaking*) Silence in court!

DOUBLEFIST (*reading*) . . . in the matter of a dispute about the
marriage of the said Figaro by the said Greenleaf, the learned
doctor Bartholo appearing for the plaintiff and the said Figaro

for himself—provided the Court allows it against the tenor of custom and the rules of the bench.

FIGARO Custom, Mister Doublefist, is often mere corruption. A party to a suit always knows his case better than some barrister who sweats without conviction and shouts his head off about everything he knows, except the facts, and who does not mind ruining the suitor, boring the court, and putting the jury to sleep. And afterwards he is as puffed up as if he had written Cicero's orations. I can put my case in two words. Gentlemen—

DOUBLEFIST Those you've uttered so far are wasted, for you are not the plaintiff. You can only defend. Come forward, doctor, and read into the evidence the promise of marriage.

FIGARO Yes, the promise.

BARTHOLO (*putting on his glasses*) It is explicit.

BRIDLEGOOSE We have to see.

DOUBLEFIST Gentlemen, please be quiet.

BEADLE (*croaking*) Silence in court!

BARTHOLO "I, the undersigned, acknowledge having received from the Damozel, etcetera, Marceline Greenleaf, of the manor of Aguas-Frescas, the sum of two thousand piastres, which sum I shall repay on her demand and in the said manor,—er—and shall marry her as a token of gratitude, etcetera, signed: Figaro—er—just Figaro. My client asks for the payment of the note and the execution of the promise, with costs. (*Pleading*) Gentlemen! Never was a more moving request brought to the bar of a Court. Since the case of Alexander the Great, who promised marriage to the beautiful Thalestris—

COUNT (*interrupting*) Before you go farther, counsel, is the genuineness of the document stipulated?

BRIDLEGOOSE (*to* FIGARO) What do you say to the f-f-facts just read into the evidence?

FIGARO I say there is malice, error, or inadvertence in the manner in which the document was read. For the statement does not say:

"Which sum I shall repay *and* I shall marry her;" it says: "Which sum I shall repay *or* I shall marry her," which is very different.

COUNT Does the document say *and* or does it say *or*?

BARTHOLO It says *and*.

FIGARO It says *or*.

BRIDLEGOOSE Doublefist, you read it.

DOUBLEFIST (*taking the paper*) That's always wise, because the parties twist things as they read. Er—er—er—"Damozel—er—Greenleaf—er—Ha! Which sum I shall repay on her demand, and in the said manor,—er—shall marry—and . . . or . . . there's *and* after demand and *o r* at the end of man*or*, but after that it's hard to make out—there is a blot.

BRIDLEGOOSE A b-blot? Ah, I und-derstand!

BARTHOLO (*pleading again*) I submit, my lord and gentlemen, that the decisive word is the copulative conjunction *and* which links the correlative members of the sentence: "I shall pay the Damozel, etcetera, *and* I shall marry her."

FIGARO (*in the same tone*) And I maintain that it is the alternative conjunction *or,* which separates the said members: "I shall pay the damsel *or* I shall marry her." To his pedantry I oppose my superpedantry: if he drops into Latin, I come up with Greek and exterminate him.

COUNT How am I to adjudicate such a question?

BARTHOLO To settle it and no longer quibble over a syllable, we stipulate the absence of the second *and,* after *manor*.

FIGARO I ask for an affidavit to that effect.

BARTHOLO We stand by our stipulation. But it affords no escape for the guilty, for let us examine the document with the stipulation in mind: "Which sum I shall repay on demand—and in the said manor shall marry her . . ." It is as if one said: "I shall have myself bled in this room—and in this bed will remain until I feel better." Or again: "He will take a dose of calomel tonight—and in the morning will experience the good effect." Thus, my lord and gentlemen, "he will repay on demand—and in the said manor will marry. . . ."

FIGARO   Nothing of the kind! There is a word under the blot and it is *or,* as thus: "Either illness carries you off, OR your physician will see to it." That is irrefutable. Another example: "Either you write wretched stuff, OR all the fools will mark you down." Does Dr. Bartholo think that I have forgotten my grammar? "I shall repay, on her demand and in the said manor COMMA or I shall marry her."

BARTHOLO *(quickly)*   There's no comma.

FIGARO *(just as quickly)*   There is. It goes: "Comma, or I shall marry her."

BARTHOLO *(glancing at the paper)*   It's without a comma.

FIGARO   It was there, my lord and gentlemen, before the blot. Besides, does a man who marries have to pay the debt as well?

BARTHOLO *(instantly)*   Yes, because we marry under a separate property agreement.

FIGARO *(just as fast)*   If marriage does not cancel the debt, we insist on the separation of persons *and* property!

         (The Judges rise and confer).

BARTHOLO   A rewarding cancellation!

DOUBLEFIST   Silence, gentlemen!

BEADLE *(croaking)*   Silence in court!

BARTHOLO   Scoundrels of this stripe call it paying their debts!

FIGARO   Are you speaking now on your own behalf?

BARTHOLO   I am defending this lady.

FIGARO   You may go on raving, but please stop casting aspersions. When the law, fearing the passions of the interested parties, allowed the intervention of counsel, it did not mean to permit these temperate defenders to become privileged slanderers. That would have been to degrade the noblest of institutions.

(*The judges are still conferring*).

ANTONIO (*to* MARCELINE *and pointing to the judges*) Why must they palaverate so long?

MARCELINE They got at the chief justice, he is getting around the other one, and I am about to lose the case.

BARTHOLO (*somberly*) I am afraid so.

FIGARO (*gaily*) Cheer up, Marceline!

DOUBLEFIST (*jumping up and addressing* MARCELINE) That's too much! I denounce you, and for the honor of the Court I ask that before the other case is settled you be tried for contempt!

COUNT (*sitting down*) No, master clerk. I shall not judge in my own case for an insult to my person. No Spanish judge will have to blush for such an abuse of power, worthy only of an oriental despot. We commit enough wrongs as it is. I am now going to correct one of these by stating the reasons for my decision. Any judge who rules and gives no reason is an enemy of the law. What does the plaintiff ask? Marriage failing payment. Both together would be contradictory.

DOUBLEFIST Silence, gentlemen!

BEADLE (*croaking*) Silence in court!

COUNT What does the defendant rejoin? That he wants to retain possession of his person. Permission is granted.

FIGARO I've won!

COUNT But since the text says: Which sum I shall repay on the first demand *or* I shall marry, etc., the Court orders the defendant to pay the plaintiff two thousand piastres *or* to marry her within the day. (*Rises*)

FIGARO (*petrified*) I've lost!

ANTONIO (*delighted*) A magnificent decision!

FIGARO How, magnificent?

ANTONIO On account of how you aren't no longer my nephew-in-law, thank the lord!

BEADLE (*croaking*) Move along, gem'mun. (*Exeunt*)

ANTONIO   I'm off to tell all about it to my niece.

MARCELINE (*sitting down*)   Now I can breathe freely.

FIGARO   But I am suffocating.

COUNT (*aside*)   And I am avenged; it's very soothing.

FIGARO (*aside*)   Where's Basil, who was supposed to prevent Marceline's marriage—he's back in good time, I don't think! (*To the* COUNT *on his way out*) Leaving us, my lord?

COUNT   There's nothing more to judge.

FIGARO (*looking at* BRIDLEGOOSE)   If it weren't for that fathead—

BRIDLEGOOSE   Me, a fathead?

FIGARO   Who can doubt it? And I shan't marry her: I am a gentleman after all. (*The* COUNT *stops*)

BARTHOLO   You will marry her.

FIGARO   Without my noble progenitors' consent?

BARTHOLO   Give us their name, exhibit them.

FIGARO   Give me a little time. I must be close to finding them, I've been looking for fifteen years.

BARTHOLO   Conceited ass! A foundling!

FIGARO   Not found, doctor, lost, or rather, stolen.

COUNT (*returning*)   Stolen, lost—where's the proof? Otherwise he'll cry out that he's being cheated.

FIGARO   My lord, even if the lace on my baby clothes, and the embroidered coverlet, and the gold and jewels I wore when the brigands snatched me, did not suffice to prove my high birth, the care that had been taken to put distinctive marks on me would show that I was a valuable offspring. I have hieroglyphics on my arm . . . (*He starts to roll up his right sleeve*)

MARCELINE (*rising quickly*)   You have a mark like a spatula on your right arm?

FIGARO   How do you know I have?

MARCELINE   Good God, it's he!

FIGARO   Of course it's me.

BARTHOLO (*to* MARCELINE)   Who?

MARCELINE (*quickly*)   It's Emmanuel!

BARTHOLO (*to* FIGARO)   You were kidnapped by gypsies?

FIGARO (*excited*)   Near a castle, yes. My good doctor, if you restore me to my noble family, set a high price on your services. Gold and treasure are trifles to my illustrious parents.

BARTHOLO (*pointing to* MARCELINE)   There is your mother.

FIGARO   Foster mother?

BARTHOLO   Your own mother.

COUNT   His mother?

FIGARO   Explain.

MARCELINE (*pointing to* BARTHOLO)   There is your father.

FIGARO (*in distress*)   Ah, oh, woe is me!

MARCELINE   Didn't the voice of nature tell you so again and again?

FIGARO   Not once.

COUNT (*aside*)   His mother!

BRIDLEGOOSE   One thing is c-c-clear: he won't marry her.*

COUNT   Stupid turn of events—most annoying!

BRIDLEGOOSE (*to* FIGARO)   And your nobility? Your castle? You would hoodwink the law with false pretenses?

FIGARO   The law! It nearly made me commit a prize blunder, the law did—on top of the fact that for those accursèd hundred pounds,** many is the time I almost beat up this gentleman who turns out to be my father. But since heaven has saved my virtue from these temptations, father of mine, please accept my apologies . . . And you, mother mine, fold me in your arms—as maternally as you can.

(MARCELINE *clasps him about the neck*).

SUZANNE (*running with a purse in her hand*)   My lord, stop

---

* At this point occurs a declamatory passage of about two pages on society's unjust treatment of women. It was omitted in the original production and has not been played since, though Beaumarchais printed it in his Preface.
** An allusion to Figaro's successful swindle of Bartholo in *The Barber of Seville*.

everything! Do not marry them: I've come to pay this lady with the dowry madam has given me.

COUNT (*aside*) The devil take the countess! It is as if everything conspired . . . (*Exit*)

ANTONIO (*seeing* FIGARO *embracing his mother, addresses* SUZANNE) Payment, eh? I see, I see.

SUZANNE (*turning her back*) I've seen enough; let's go, uncle.

FIGARO Please don't! What is it you've seen enough?

SUZANNE My weakness of mind and your lack of integrity—

FIGARO Neither of them a fact.

SUZANNE (*angrily*) —and your willingness to marry her and caress her.

FIGARO (*gaily*) I caress but don't marry. (SUZANNE *tries to leave;* FIGARO *prevents her;* SUZANNE *slaps him*)

SUZANNE You are impertinent and rude, let me go!

FIGARO (*to the company*) That's love for you! Before you go, though, I beg you take a good look at the dear woman in front of you.

SUZANNE I'm looking.

FIGARO How does she strike you?

SUZANNE Horrible!

FIGARO Long live jealousy! No half measures about it.

MARCELINE (*arms open to* SUZANNE) Come kiss your mother, my pretty Suzanette. The naughty boy who is tormenting you is my son.

SUZANNE (*running to her*) You—his mother! (*They stay clasped in each other's arms*)

ANTONIO It must have just happened.

FIGARO No, only just disclosed.

MARCELINE (*with fervor*) My heart was right to be so strongly drawn to him, though mistaking its reason. Blood was speaking to me.

FIGARO And good sense to me, which worked like instinct, to make me refuse you. For I was far from hating you, witness the money. . . .

MARCELINE (*handing him a paper*) The money is yours: take back your note. It is your dowry.

SUZANNE (*throwing the purse to him*) And take this too!

FIGARO Many thanks!

MARCELINE (*excited*) I was unfortunate as a girl, and just now was about to become the most wretched of wives; I am now the happiest of mothers. Come kiss me, children: all my feelings of love are centered upon you. I am as happy as anyone can be and —oh, children, how I am going to love you!

FIGARO (*moved and speaking with vehemence*) Please stop, dearest mother, or you will see my eyes dissolve away in the first tears I have ever shed. They are tears of joy—but what a fool I am: I nearly felt ashamed of myself as I felt the drops on my hands. (*He shows his hands, fingers outspread.*) I stupidly tried to hold them back. Away, false shame! I want to laugh and cry all at once. What I now feel does not come to a man twice in a lifetime. (*He kisses his mother to one side of him,* SUZANNE *on the other*)

MARCELINE Oh, my dear!

SUZANNE My very dear!

BRIDLEGOOSE (*wiping his eyes*) It seems I am a f-fool also!

FIGARO (*excited*) Grief! I can now defy you: afflict me if you can, between these two women I love.

ANTONIO (*to* FIGARO) Not so many pretty speeches, if you please. Apropos of marriage, in good families, that of the parents is supposed to precede. Do your parents ask each other's hand?

BARTHOLO May my hand rot and fall off if I ever offer it to the mother of such a character!

ANTONIO (*to* BARTHOLO) In other words you're nothing but an unnatural father? (*To* FIGARO) In that case, Lothario, the bargain's off.

SUZANNE   Oh, uncle!

ANTONIO   D'you think I'll give my sister's child to this here who's no one's child?

BRIDLEGOOSE   How do you make that out, idiot? Everyone is somebody's child!

ANTONIO   Yah, yah: he shan't have her nohow. (*Exit*)

BARTHOLO (*to* FIGARO)   Better look for somebody to adopt you.

(*He tries to go, but* MARCELINE *seizes him around the middle and pulls him back*).

MARCELINE   One moment, doctor, don't go.

FIGARO (*aside*)   It's incredible but all the fools in Andalusia are rabid against my poor desire to get married.

SUZANNE (*to* BARTHOLO)   Dear little father, he is your son.

MARCELINE   He has wit, talent, and presence.

FIGARO   And he never cost you a penny.

BARTHOLO   What about the hundred pounds he robbed me of?

MARCELINE (*cuddling him*)   We'll take such good care of you, papa! *

SUZANNE (*cuddling*)   We'll love you so much, dear little papa!

BARTHOLO (*yielding*)   "Papa, papa, dear papa—" Now I'm going to be as big a fool as this gentleman (*pointing to* BRIDLEGOOSE). I'm being led like a child. (MARCELINE *and* SUZANNE *kiss him*) Now, now, I haven't said Yes. (*Turning around*) What's become of his lordship?

FIGARO   Let's join him, quick, and force a decision from him. If he were to think up some new scheme, we'd have to start all over again.

ALL TOGETHER   Let's go, let's go! (*They drag* BARTHOLO *outside*)

BRIDLEGOOSE (*left alone*)   "As big a fool as this gentleman." A man can say that sort of thing about himself, but . . . they're not at all p-polite in this p-place. (*Exit*)

* Accent on the second syllable, as in mamma later.

ACT 4

A large room with candelabra all lighted, floral decorations, and other ornaments indicative of preparations for a party. Downstage right stands a table and on it a writing case. Behind the table is an armchair.

FIGARO (*hugging* SUZANNE) Well, love, are you happy? She got round the doctor, didn't she, my silver-tongued mother? Despite his distaste he is marrying her, and your curmudgeon of an uncle can't help himself. That leaves only my lord in a rage; for after all, our marriage is the upshot of theirs. What a happy ending! Aren't you inclined to laugh?

SUZANNE I never knew anything so odd.

FIGARO Say rather so jolly. All we wanted was a dowry, squeezed out of his Excellency. Now we have two which owe nothing to him. A relentless rival was hounding you and I was bedeviled by a fury. That trouble has for us both taken the form of a loving mother. Yesterday I was, so to speak, alone in the world; today I have all my relatives complete about me. True, they're not so resplendent as if I had designed them myself, but good enough for us who haven't the ambition to be rich.

SUZANNE And yet none of the things that you planned and we expected came through.

FIGARO Chance did a better job, my sweet. That's the way of the world. You toil, you scheme, you make projects, all in your own corner; Fortune works in another. From the insatiable conqueror who would like to swallow the globe to the peaceable blind man led by his dog, all human beings are the playthings of fate. Indeed, the blind man is often better served by his dog, less deceived in his opinions, than some other self-blinded man with his retinue. As for that delightful blind fellow called Love . . . (*He again embraces her tenderly*)

SUZANNE He's the only one I care about.

FIGARO Well then, let me be the serviceable dog in folly's employ, who makes it his job to lead him to your charming little door. And there we'll be cozy for the rest of our lives.

SUZANNE (*laughing*) Love and you?

FIGARO I and Love.

SUZANNE And you won't look for other lodgings?

FIGARO If you catch me at it, I'm willing to have a hundred million philanderers—

SUZANNE You're going to say more than you mean: tell me the honest truth.

FIGARO My truest truth?

SUZANNE Shame on you, rascal! Is there more than one?

FIGARO I should say so! Ever since it has been observed that with the passage of time old follies turn into wisdom, and that early little lies, even though poorly planted, bloom into great big truths —ever since then, there have been endless species of truths. There are those one dare not utter, for not every truth is fit to say; there are those one flaunts without putting faith in them, for not every truth is fit to believe. And then there are the passionate promises, the parental threats, the resolutions of drinkers, the assurances of office holders, the "positively final offers" of business men—there's no end to them. Only my love for my Suzy is true coin.

SUZANNE   I love your gaiety because it is wild. It shows you are happy. But let's talk about meeting the Count in the garden.

FIGARO   Far better never speak of that again. It nearly cost me my Sue.

SUZANNE   You don't want me to go through with it?

FIGARO   If you love me, Suzy, give me your word on this. Let him eat his heart out—it'll be his punishment.

SUZANNE   I found it harder at first to agree to it than now to give it up—I'll never mention it again.

FIGARO   That's your truest truth?

SUZANNE   I'm not like you learned people. I have only one truth.

FIGARO   And you'll love me a little?

SUZANNE   Much.

FIGARO   That isn't much.

SUZANNE   What do you mean?

FIGARO   Why, in love, don't you see, too much is barely enough.

SUZANNE   Your subtleties are beyond me, but I intend to love only my husband.

FIGARO   Stick to it and you will represent a remarkable exception to the rule. (*Starts to kiss her. Enter* COUNTESS)

COUNTESS   I was just saying: wherever they happen to be, you may be sure they're together. I really think, Figaro, that each time you indulge in a tête-à-tête you are living off the future, drawing on wedded bliss, and robbing yourself. People look for you and get impatient.

FIGARO   You are right, madam. I was forgetting myself. I will show them my excuse. (*He tries to take* SUZANNE *with him*)

COUNTESS (*holding her back*) She'll follow later (*He goes.*

COUNTESS *to* SUZANNE) Have you what's needed to change clothes with me?

SUZANNE   Nothing is needed, madam. The assignation is off.

COUNTESS   You have changed your mind?

SUZANNE   It's Figaro—

COUNTESS   You are deceiving me.

SUZANNE   God is my witness!

COUNTESS   Figaro is not a man to let a dowry slip from his grasp.

SUZANNE   Oh, madam, what can you be thinking?

COUNTESS   Why, that in concert with the Count, you are now sorry you made me privy to his plans. I can read you like a book. Leave me to myself. (*She starts to leave*)

SUZANNE (*on her knees*)   In the name of heaven which is our hope, you cannot know the wrong you do me. When you have been so endlessly good to me, after the dowry you've given me, how could I—

COUNTESS (*lifting her up*)   But—of course! I must have been out of my mind. Since you are changing places with me, dear heart, you won't be going into the garden. You'll be keeping your word to your husband and helping me recapture mine.

SUZANNE   Oh how you upset me!

COUNTESS   I've been terribly scatterbrained. (*Kisses* SUZANNE, *on the forehead*) Where is the meeting place?

SUZANNE (*kisses the Countess's hand*)   All I heard was "garden."

COUNTESS (*motioning* SUZANNE *to the table*)   Take that pen and we will name a spot.

SUZANNE   I, write to him?

COUNTESS   You must.

SUZANNE   But at least, madam, you—

COUNTESS   I'll take the responsibility for everything.

     (SUZANNE *sits at the table*).

COUNTESS (*dictating*)   "A new song to the tune of . . . : 'How lovely under the elms at night, How lovely . . .' "

SUZANNE (*writing*) ". . . under the elms" Yes, nothing else?

COUNTESS Have you the slightest fear that he won't understand?

SUZANNE You're right. (*She folds the note*) What sort of seal?

COUNTESS A pin, quick—it will serve to reply with. Write on the back: "Please return the seal."

SUZANNE (*laughing*) Ho! the seal! This seal, my lady, is a funnier joke than the one on the officer's commission.

COUNTESS (*in painful recollection*) Oh!

SUZANNE (*looking on her person*) I haven't a pin on me.

COUNTESS (*unpinning her collar*) Take this. (*The page's ribbon falls from her bosom*) Oh, my ribbon!

SUZANNE (*picking it up*) Ah, the little thief's property . . . and you were cruel enough to—

COUNTESS Could I let him wear it on his arm? A fine spectacle! Give it back to me.

SUZANNE Your ladyship cannot wear it: it is spotted with the young man's blood.

COUNTESS It will be just right for Fanchette . . . when she next brings me flowers.

> (*Enter a young shepherdess,* CHERUBINO *dressed as a girl,* FANCHETTE *and other girls dressed like her and carrying bouquets*).

FANCHETTE My lady, these girls from the village bring you flowers.

COUNTESS (*quickly hides the ribbon again*) They are delightful. It grieves me, dears, not to know you all by name. (*Pointing to* CHERUBINO) But who is this lovely child who seems so shy?

SHEPHERDESS A cousin of mine, ma'am, come to visit for the wedding.

COUNTESS So pretty! Since I can't wear all twenty of your posies, I'll honor the stranger. (*She takes* CHERUBINO's *bouquet and kisses him on the forehead*). She's blushing. Suzy, don't you think she looks like someone we know?

SUZANNE So much so I can hardly tell them apart.

CHERUBINO (*aside, both hands on his heart*) Oh, that kiss went right through me!

ANTONIO (*entering with the* COUNT) And I tell you he's here somewhere. They dressed him at my daughter's, all the clothes are still around, and here's his regulation hat, which I picked out of the lot. (*Steps forward, scans the girls' faces and recognizes* CHERUBINO, *whose female bonnet he pulls off. As* CHERUBINO'*s long hair falls in ringlets,* ANTONIO *tosses the military hat on top*) By gum, there's your officer!

COUNTESS (*stepping back*) Heavens!

SUZANNE The rapscallion!

ANTONIO I was telling you upstairs it was him.

COUNT (*angry*) Well, madam?

COUNTESS Well, sir, you find me as surprised as you and equally angry.

COUNT It may be, but what about this morning?

COUNTESS I should be guilty indeed if I kept up the deception any longer. He had dropped in to see me, and it was then we undertook the practical joke which these children have completed. You discovered Suzanne and me dressing him up. You are so quick to anger that he ran away, I lost my good judgment, and general dismay did the rest.

COUNT (*disgruntled*) Why haven't you left?

CHERUBINO (*flinging off the hat*) My lord—

COUNT I shall punish you for disobeying.

FANCHETTE (*thoughtlessly*) Oh, my lord, please listen to me: every time you come by and kiss me you always say: "Fanchette, dear, if you will love me, I'll give you anything you want."

COUNT (*flushing*) I have said that?

FANCHETTE Yes, my lord. Well, instead of punishing Cherubino, give him to me for a husband, and then I'll love you madly.

COUNT (*aside*) Diddled by a page!

COUNTESS   Count, it is your turn now. This child's naïve confession, as innocent as mine, bears witness to a double truth, which is that when I cause you anguish it is always unintentionally, whereas you do your utmost to increase and justify my own.

ANTONIO   You too my lord? By gum, I'm going to get after that chit as I did after her mother, now gathered. . . . Not that it's of consequence, but as my lady knows, these little girls when they grow up. . . .

COUNT (*discomfited, aside*)   There is an evil genius in this place who turns everything against me.

FIGARO (*entering*)   My lord, if you detain the young ladies, the party can't begin, or the dance either.

COUNT   You want to dance? Have you forgotten how you fell this morning and sprained your right foot?

FIGARO (*swinging his leg*)   It's still a trifle sore, but it's nothing. (*To the girls*) Come along, darlings, come.

COUNT (*turning* FIGARO *about*)   You were lucky the flowerbed was soft earth.

FIGARO   Very lucky—otherwise . . .

ANTONIO (*twists him the other way*)   Besides he "gathered himself together" as he fell all the way to the bottom.

FIGARO   A really clever man would have stopped halfway down. (*To the girls*) Are you coming, ladies?

ANTONIO (*twisting* FIGARO *again*)   All the while the little page was galloping on his horse toward Seville.

FIGARO   Galloping, or maybe sauntering. . . .

COUNT (*twists* FIGARO *the other way*)   And his commission was in your pocket.

FIGARO (*somewhat surprised*)   Undoubtedly, but why this examination? (*To the girls*) Now come on, girls!

ANTONIO (*pulling* CHERUBINO *by the arm*)   Here's one who says my future nephew is a liar.

FIGARO (*taken aback*)   Cherubino! (*Aside*) Blast the little braggart!

ANTONIO   Have you got it now?

FIGARO   Got it, got it! . . . By the by, what's his story?

COUNT (*drily*)   Hardly a story, he says it was he who jumped into the gillyflowers.

FIGARO (*abstracted*)   Hm, if he says so . . . it may well be. I don't argue about what I don't know.

COUNT   So both you and he . . .

FIGARO   Why not? The jumping fever is catching—just think of sheep over a fence.* And when my lord is angry, anyone would prefer to risk his neck—

COUNT   Now really, two by two?

FIGARO   We'd have done it by the dozen—and why should you care, my lord, seeing no one was hurt? (*To the girls*) I say, are you coming in or aren't you?

COUNT (*outraged*)   Is it a farce we're playing together, you and I?

          (*Music begins offstage*).

FIGARO   There's the opening march. Fall in, my beauties, fall in. Here, Suzanne, give me your arm.

          (*Exeunt except* CHERUBINO *who stays behind, his head hung down*).

COUNT (*gazing at* FIGARO's *back*)   Did you ever see greater nerve? (*To* CHERUBINO) As for you, sly boots who now pretend to be ashamed, go dress yourself properly and let me not see your face for the rest of the evening.

COUNTESS   He will be terribly bored.

CHERUBINO (*thoughtlessly*)   Bored? I carry on my brow enough happiness to outweigh a hundred years in jail! (*He puts on his hat and leaves*)

---

* In the original Beaumarchais refers to the sheep in Rabelais which Panurge induced to jump overboard by throwing over the first one.

COUNTESS (*fans herself violently*)

COUNT What is so happy about his brow?

COUNTESS (*embarrassed*) His first military hat, I suppose. With children any novelty is like a toy. (*She starts to leave*)

COUNT You won't stay, Countess?

COUNTESS I told you I did not feel well.

COUNT One moment more for the sake of your protégée—or I'll think you are cross.

COUNTESS Here come the two wedding processions. Let us sit and receive them.

COUNT (*aside*) The wedding! . . . Well, what can't be cured must be endured. (COUNT *and* COUNTESS *sit to one side of the room.*

Enter the processions to a march based on the Folies d'Espagne: *

A gamekeeper, a musket on his shoulder

The mayor, the aldermen, BRIDLEGOOSE

Peasants and their women in party dress

Two young girls carrying the virgin's bonnet

Two others in white veils

Two others, wearing gloves and a corsage at the waist

ANTONIO *holding* SUZANNE'S *hand to give her away to* FIGARO

Other girls with other types of bonnets and veils

MARCELINE *wearing a white veil and bonnet similar to the first.*

FIGARO *holding* MARCELINE'S *hand to give her away to:*

The doctor, who brings up the rear of the procession, wearing a large boutonniere.

The girls, as they pass in front of the COUNT, *deliver to his footmen the paraphernalia for* SUZANNE *and* MARCELINE.

The peasants, men and women, in two lines, dance the fandango to an accompaniment of castanets. Then the

---

* Presumed to be an old Spanish dance, but known to us only through a theme in ¾ time called Follia in Corelli's *Solos,* op. 5 and used also by Vivaldi and others. *Folies* here does not imply folly but foliage, as in *Folies Bergère.*

orchestra plays the introduction of the duet, during which
ANTONIO *takes* SUZANNE *to the* COUNT. *She kneels before
him, he puts the virgin's bonnet on her head, and gives her
a bouquet. During this ceremony the girls sing the following duet:*

Sing, young bride, the grateful benefaction!
Your master has his selfish lust displaced:
He gives up pleasure for a noble action,
And to your husband hands you pure and chaste.

As the duet concludes, SUZANNE, *still kneeling, tugs at the*
COUNT'S *cloak and shows him the note she has for him. She
then puts her hand to her hair and he takes the note while
seeming to adjust her bonnet. He puts the note inside his
coat, the duet ends,* SUZANNE *rises and makes a low curtsy.*
FIGARO *receives* SUZANNE *from the hand of the* COUNT *and
steps back with her to the other end of the room, near* MAR-
CELINE. *There is meanwhile a reprise of the fandango. The*
COUNT, *being in a hurry to read his note, comes downstage
and pulls the paper from his pocket. The pin evidently
pricks him, for he shakes his finger, squeezes it, and licks it.
He looks at the folded paper and speaks.*

COUNT The devil take all women! They stick pins into everything.

(*He throws the pin on the ground, reads the note and kisses
it. While he and* FIGARO *speak, the orchestra plays pianis-
simo.* FIGARO, *who has seen the by-play, speaks to* SUZANNE
and his mother).

FIGARO It must be a billet-doux some little wench slipped into
his hand as she walked by. It was sealed with a pin which impu-
dently pricked him.

(*The dance resumes. The* COUNT *turns the note over and*

sees the request to return the pin. He looks for it on the ground, finds it, and sticks it in his sleeve).

FIGARO (*to* SUZANNE *and* MARCELINE) From the beloved any object is dear, so he's retrieved the pin. What a harlequin he is!

(*Meanwhile,* SUZANNE *and the* COUNTESS *have been exchanging signals. The dance concludes and the introduction of the duet is played again.* FIGARO *takes* MARCELINE *to the* COUNT, *and the ceremony repeats. But just as the* COUNT *lifts the bonnet and as the duet strikes up, the proceedings are interrupted by a great noise at the door).*

FOOTMAN Keep back, keep back, gentlemen, you can't all get in together. Help here! the guards! (*Guards step quickly toward the door*)

COUNT (*rising*) What is the matter there?

FOOTMAN My lord, it is Mister Basil who is followed by the whole township because he sings as he walks.

COUNT Admit him alone.

COUNTESS Please command me to withdraw.

COUNT I shan't forget your obliging me.

COUNTESS Suzanne! . . . (*To the* COUNT) She will be back at once. (*Aside, to* SUZANNE) Let's go change our clothes.

(*Exeunt*).

MARCELINE He never shows up but to do harm.

FIGARO You see if I don't change his tune.

(*Enter* BASIL, *guitar in hand, followed by* SUNSTRUCK).

BASIL (*sings to the music of the final song of the play*)

> Faithful, tender, loving hearts
> Who condemn love's wanderings
> Do not launch your angry darts;
> It is not a crime to change,
> For if Cupid carries wings

It must be to flit and range!
It must be to flit and range!

FIGARO (*going toward* BASIL) Yes, that's the reason precisely why Love has wings on his back. Friend, what do you mean by your song?

BASIL (*pointing to* SUNSTRUCK) I mean that after showing submissiveness to my lord and entertaining this gentleman, who is of my lord's company, I want to claim my lord's justice.

SUNSTRUCK Pah, your lordsy, he didn't entertain me at all—he just had fits of yodeling!

COUNT What is it you want, Basil?

BASIL That which already belongs to me, my lord—the hand of Marceline.

FIGARO (*drawing near*) How long has it been since you saw the face of a lunatic?

BASIL My good sir, I see one right now.

FIGARO Since you use my eyes as a mirror, study the effect therein of the prophecy I am about to make: if you so much as seem to gravitate toward madame—

BARTHOLO (*laughing*) But why? Let him speak.

BRIDLEGOOSE (*coming forward*) Is it n-necessary for two old f-friends . . .

FIGARO He and I friends?

BASIL Absurd!

FIGARO (*setting a rapid pace for the ensuing dialogue*) Friends because he writes the dullest church music?

BASIL While he writes newspaper verse?

FIGARO A tavern musician!

BASIL A penny-a-liner!

FIGARO An oratorio-monger!

BASIL A diplomatic nag!

COUNT (*seated*)   Vulgarians both!

BASIL   He's failed me at every turn.

FIGARO   That's an idea I wish were true.

BASIL   He goes round calling me an ass.

FIGARO   Don't mistake me for public opinion.

BASIL   Whereas there's hardly a talented singer I haven't trained.

FIGARO   Strained!

BASIL   He persists!

FIGARO   And why shouldn't I, if I speak the truth? Are you a prince that you should be flattered? Learn to live with the truth, faker! It's certain no liar could make much of you. Perhaps you're afraid the truth will come out of our mouths? If so, why did you interrupt our nuptials?

BASIL (*to* MARCELINE)   Did you or did you not promise me that if you weren't provided for within four years, you would give me your hand?

MARCELINE   Under what condition did I promise this?

BASIL   That if you found your lost child, I would adopt him out of kindness to you.

ALL (*together*)   He's been found!

BASIL   All right, I'm ready.

ALL (*together, pointing to* FIGARO)   There he is!

BASIL (*shrinking back*)   Get thee behind me!

BRIDLEGOOSE   That means you g-give up his d-dear mother?

BASIL   What could be worse than to be thought the father of such a fellow?

FIGARO   Why, to be thought your son! You're pulling my leg!

BASIL (*pointing to* FIGARO)   The moment this character is somebody in this house, I want everyone to know that I am nobody. (*Exit*)

BARTHOLO (*laughing*)   Hahahaha!

FIGARO (*leaping with joy*)   At last, at last, I'll have my bride!

COUNT (*aside*)   And I my mistress. (*He rises*)

BRIDLEGOOSE (*to* MARCELINE)   With everybody s-satisfied.

COUNT   Let the two marriage contracts be drawn up. I shall sign them.

ALL (*together*)   Bravo!

COUNT   I need time to myself. (*He starts to leave with the others*)

SUNSTRUCK (*to* FIGARO)   Now I'm going to set up the fireworks under the elms as I was told.

COUNT (*coming back*)   What idiot gave you that order?

FIGARO   What's wrong with it?

COUNT   Why, the Countess is indisposed. How can she see the display from indoors unless it's on the terrace, below her room?

FIGARO   You heard him, Sunstruck? On the terrace.

COUNT   Under the elms, the idea! (*Leaving, aside*) They were going to set fire to my tête-à-tête.

FIGARO   What considerateness for his wife! (*Starts to leave*)

MARCELINE (*stopping him*)   A word with you, my son. I owe you an apology. Mistaken feeling for you made me unjust to your wife: I thought her in league with the Count, even though Basil had told me she always rejected his advances.

FIGARO   You don't know your son if you think that female whims and wiles can shake him. I challenge the cleverest to upset me.

MARCELINE   It's nice to feel that way, at any rate, because jealousy—

FIGARO   Is but a stupid child of pride, or else it's a madman's disease. I assure you, mother, on this point I'm a philosopher—unshakable. So if Suzanne ever deceives me, I forgive her in advance, for she will have worked hard and long to do it. (*He turns and sees* FANCHETTE *who is looking everywhere for someone*)

FIGARO   So-o, little cousin! Getting an earful?

FANCHETTE   Oh, no! I was brought up to think it's not nice.

FIGARO   True enough, but since it's useful, it's often considered worth the trouble.

FANCHETTE   I was finding out if somebody was here.

FIGARO   So young and so full of guile! You know perfectly well he can't be here.

FANCHETTE   Who's that?

FIGARO   Cherubino.

FANCHETTE   It isn't he I'm after. I know where *he* is. It's cousin Sue.

FIGARO   And what do you want with her?

FANCHETTE   I can tell *you,* because you're my cousin now. It's about a pin I'm supposed to give her.

FIGARO (*startled*)   A pin? A pin did you say? And from whom, you little hussy? At your age you're already in the business of— (*He catches himself and goes on gently*) You're already pretty good at whatever you do, Fanchette; and my pretty cousin is so obliging that—

FANCHETTE   What did I do to make you cross with me? I'm going . . .

FIGARO   Don't. I was only teasing. I'll tell you: that pin of yours is one that my lord told you to give to Suzanne. It's the one that fastened the paper he had in his hand: you see I know what I'm talking about.

FANCHETTE   Why ask me if you know?

FIGARO (*fumbling*)   Oh . . . because it's fun to know how his lordship went about sending you on your errand.

FANCHETTE (*with naïveté*)   Well, he did it almost as you say: "Here, Fanchette," he said, "give back this pin to your beautiful cousin; just tell her it's the seal for the big elms."

FIGARO   "The big—?

FANCHETTE   "—elms." Oh, yes, and he added: "Be sure no one sees you."

FIGARO   Well, cousin, you must do as you're told and it's lucky no one *has* seen you. Run your pretty errand and don't tell Suzanne a word more than his lordship told you.

FANCHETTE Why should I say more, cousin? He takes me for a child. (*She goes out skipping*)

FIGARO Well, mother?

MARCELINE Well, my son?

FIGARO (*choking*) That cursèd clown! Really some things are too much!

MARCELINE Some things, what things?

FIGARO (*hands on his breast*) What I've just learned, mother, weighs on me like lead—here.

MARCELINE (*laughing*) It would seem that your assured countenance of a while ago was only an inflated bag of wind—a pin has made it collapse.

FIGARO (*furious*) But that pin, mother, that pin was the one he picked up!

MARCELINE (*recalling his words*) "As for jealousy, I am a philosopher—unshakable: if Suzanne deceives me, I forgive her . . ."

FIGARO Oh, mother, a man speaks as he feels at the time. Let the coolest judge on the bench plead his own case and see how he explains the law. I understand now why he was annoyed about the fireworks. As for my darling and her subtlety with pins, she hasn't got where she thinks she is, elms or no elms. It's true my marriage is enough to warrant my anger, but it isn't enough to keep me from dropping one wife and wedding another.

MARCELINE A spendid conclusion! Let's wreck everything on a mere suspicion. How do you know it's you she's deceiving and not the Count? Have you studied her thoroughly that you condemn her without appeal? Do you know for a fact that she is going under those trees, or what her intention is, or what she will say and do if she goes there? I thought you had more judgment!

FIGARO (*kissing her hand*) A mother is always right, mother, and you are right, entirely right! But make allowance, dear mamma, for natural impulse. One feels better after giving way to it. Now let us weigh before accusing and acting. I know where the assignation is to be. Farewell, mother. (*Exit*)

MARCELINE　Farewell. And I too know where it is. Now that I've stopped him, I'd better look after Suzanne—or rather, give her warning. She is such a pretty creature! I must say, when our own interest does not divide us, we women are all inclined to make common cause in defense of our downtrodden sex against this proud, terrifying (*laughing*) and somewhat slow-witted masculine sex. (*Exit*)

ACT 5

*A stand of elms in the park. Two pavilions, kiosks, or gar-
den temples occupy respectively the right and left middle
ground. Behind is a clearing hung with decorations; in
front a lawn with seats. The scene is dark.*

FANCHETTE (*alone and carrying in one hand two small cakes and
an orange; in the other, a lighted paper lantern*) He said the
pavilion on the left. It must be this one. But what if my fine
fellow doesn't show up? They wouldn't even give me an orange
and two cookies, those kitchen people. "But for whom, miss?"
"Why, sir, it's for somebody." "We thought as much, miss." Supposing the worst—just because my lord doesn't want to set eyes on
him, that's no reason he should starve. All the same, it cost me a
big kiss on the cheek. Who knows, maybe he'll pay me back for it
in kind. (*She catches sight of* FIGARO *who comes forward to iden-*

tify her. She cries out) Ah! . . . (*Runs away and enters pavilion at left*)

FIGARO (*in a large cloak, alone at first*) It's Fanchette! (*He scans the others as they arrive and speaks roughly to them*) Good day, gentlemen, good evening. Are you all here?

BASIL All those you asked to come.

FIGARO What time is it, about?

ANTONIO (*nose in the air*) The moon should be up.

BARTHOLO What black arts are you getting ready for? He looks like a conspirator.

FIGARO Isn't it for a wedding that you're gathered at the castle?

BRIDLEGOOSE C-certainly.

ANTONIO We were going over yonder, in the park, and wait for the signal to start the festivities.

FIGARO You shan't go a step farther. It's here, under the elms, that we're going to celebrate the faithful bride I am marrying and the faithful lord who has reassigned her to himself.

BASIL (*recalling the day's events*) Ah, yes. I know all about it. Let's remove ourselves, if you please. It's a matter of a rendez-vous. I'll tell you about it later.

BRIDLEGOOSE (*to* FIGARO) We'll c-come back.

FIGARO When you hear me call, don't fail to appear. You can curse me if I don't provide you with a fine spectacle.

BARTHOLO Remember that a wise man does not start a quarrel with the great and powerful.

FIGARO I'll remember.

BARTHOLO They begin with a score of forty-love against us, thanks to their rank.

FIGARO To say nothing of their capacity for hard work, which you're forgetting. But remember also that once a man is known to be scared, he's at the mercy of every scoundrel.

BARTHOLO Well said.

FIGARO   And among my names is Greenleaf, from my mother's side.

BARTHOLO   He is full of the devil.

BRIDLEGOOSE   He y-y-is.

BASIL (*aside*)   The Count and Suzanne planned this without me—I'm rather glad of this ambush.

FIGARO (*to the footmen*)   You fellows do as I told you—light up all around here, or in the name of Death, which I'd like to throttle, when I grab the arm of one of you—(*He grabs* SUN-STRUCK)

SUNSTRUCK (*goes off crying*)   Ah, oh, ah, perish the brute!

BASIL (*leaving*)   God give you joy, young newlywed!

FIGARO (*pacing up and down alone in the dark and speaking in sombre tones*)   Oh, woman, woman, woman! weak and deceitful creature! No animal on earth can go against instinct; is it yours to deceive? After refusing me stubbornly when I begged her in front of her mistress—in the very instant of plighting her troth to me, in the middle of the ceremony—He was laughing as he read, the traitor! And I like a poor booby . . . No, my lord Count, you shan't have her, you shan't! Because you are a great lord you think you are a great genius. Nobility, wealth, honors, emoluments —it all makes a man so proud! What have you done to earn so many advantages? You took the trouble to be born, nothing more. Apart from that, you're a rather common type. Whereas I—by God!—lost in the nameless herd, I had to exert more strategy and skill merely to survive than has been spent for a hundred years in governing the Spanish Empire. . . . And you want to tangle with me!

Someone's coming—it is she—no, it's nobody. The night is dark as pitch and here am I plying the silly trade of husband, even though I'm only half of one. (*He sits on a bench*) Can anything be stranger than my career? The son of God knows whom, stolen by bandits and reared in their ways, I become disgusted and try to lead an honest life. Everywhere I am repulsed. I learn chemistry, pharmacy, surgery, yet the whole influence of a great lord hardly succeeds in securing me the practice of a veterinary. Tired of pestering sick animals, hoping in fact to do just the opposite, I go headlong for the stage. Far better have hung a millstone around my neck! I write a play satirizing life in the harem: being a Spanish author I thought I could make fun of Mohammed without fear. At once, an emissary from God knows where complains that my verses offend the Sublime Porte, Persia, part of the Indian peninsula, all of Egypt, the kingdoms of Barca, Tripoli, Tunis, Algiers, and Morocco—and there goes my play up the spout, to please the Mohammedan princes, not one of whom (I believe) can read, and all of whom brand us on the shoulder and call us Christian dogs. Whoever fails to degrade the mind avenges himself by insulting it. My cheeks were growing hollow, my lodging was unpaid, I could see from afar the threatening bailiff with a pen stuck in his wig, so I shudder and exert myself afresh. A public debate starts up about the nature of wealth, and since one needn't own something in order to argue about it, being in fact penniless, I write on the value of money and interest. Immediately, I find myself inside a coach looking at the drawbridge of a prison and leaving hope and freedom behind. (*He gets up*) How I should like to hold in the hollow of my hand one of these potentates who last four days in office and are ready to ordain punishments! When a healthy fall from grace had sobered his pride, I'd let him know that printed nonsense is dangerous only in countries where its free circulation is hampered; that without the right to criticize, praise and approval are worthless, and that only petty men fear petty writings. (*Sits down*) One day, tired of feeding an obscure guest, they threw me out into the street, and since a man must eat even when out of jail, I sharpen my quill once more and ask people what is in the news. I am told that during my retreat at public expense, free trade and a free press have been established in Madrid, so that, provided I do not write about the government, or about religion, or politics, or morals, or those in power, or public bodies, or the Opera, or the other state theatres, or about anybody who is active in anything, I can print whatever I want with perfect freedom under the supervision of two or three censors. To take advantage of such sweet liberty, I let it be known that I am starting a periodical, and to make sure that I am not treading on anybody's heels, I call it *The Useless Journal*. Mercy! No sooner done than I see a thousand poor devils of subsidized hacks in arms against me. I am put down and once again unemployed. Despair nearly had me by the throat when someone thought of me for a vacant place. Unfortunately I was qualified for it. They needed an accountant and put in a dancer. The only way out was to turn thief. I set up as croupier of a gambling den. Ah, then, my dears, I was in the swim! I dine out and people known as respectable courteously open their houses to me, keeping for themselves only three quarters of the take. I could have recouped all my losses —I had even begun to understand that to grow rich, know-how is better than knowledge, but since everyone around me was robbing the till while requiring that I stay honest, I went under for the third time.

I'd had enough and meant to break with the world—five fathoms of water would suffice, and nearly did, when my guardian angel recalled me to my original trade. I take up my razors and lancet and leave glory to the fools who feed on its aroma. With it also, I leave behind dishonor, which is too heavy a load for a pedestrian. Hiking from town to town, shaving as I go, I live at last a life without care. But a great lord passing through Seville recognizes me. I get him married off, and as a reward for my helping him secure a wife, he now wants to intercept mine. Thereupon, storms and intrigues. I am on the edge of an abyss, nearly wedded to my own mother, when lo! my relatives materialize,

Indian file. (*He gets up and grows vehement*) Follows a regular scrimmage—"it's he, it's you, it's I. No, it isn't, not I." Well, who then? (*He falls back into the seat*). What an incredible series of events! How did it happen to *me*? Why these things and not others? Who drew them down on my head? Forcibly set on the road of life, not knowing where it leads, and bound to leave it against my will, I've tried to keep it as rosy as my natural cheerfulness permits. Here again I say *my* cheerfulness without knowing if it belongs to me any more than those other things; nor do I know who this *I* may be with which I am so concerned—it's first a shapeless collection of unknown parts, then a helpless puny thing, then a lively little animal, then a young man thirsting for pleasure, with a full capacity to enjoy and ready to use any shifts to live— master here and valet there, at the whim of fortune; ambitious from vanity, industrious from need—and lazy . . . with delight! An orator in tight spots, a poet for relaxation, a musician from time to time, a lover in hot fits: I have seen everything, done everything, worn out everything. At last my illusion is shattered and I'm now wholly disabused . . . blasé, . . . Oh Suzy! Suzy! my Suzy, what torments you are putting me through! I hear footsteps . . . someone's coming . . . This is the crisis. (*He retires into the downstage wing on his right*)

> (*Enter the* COUNTESS *dressed as* SUZANNE, SUZANNE *dressed as the* COUNTESS, *and* MARCELINE).

SUZANNE (*speaking low to the* COUNTESS) Yes, Marceline said Figaro would be here.

MARCELINE And so he is; be quiet.

SUZANNE I see; the one's eavesdropping, the other's coming to fetch me—let the show begin.

MARCELINE I don't want to miss a word; I'm going to hide in the pavilion. (*Enters the same pavilion as* FANCHETTE)

SUZANNE (*aloud*) You're trembling, madam: are you cold?

COUNTESS (*aloud*) The evening is damp, I am going in.

SUZANNE (*aloud*)   If my lady does not need me, I should like to take the air a little while under the trees.

COUNTESS (*aloud*)   Take the air! catch your death, you mean.

SUZANNE   I'm used to it.

FIGARO (*aside*)   Her death, my eye! (SUZANNE *retreats to a spot near the wings, on the opposite side from* FIGARO)

CHERUBINO (*dressed as an officer, comes on singing the words of his song*)   "Tra-la-la-la-la, A godmother I had, Whom always I adored!"

COUNTESS (*aside*)   The little page!

CHERUBINO   People are walking about. I must take to my refuge, where Fanchette is—oh, it's a woman!

COUNTESS   Oh, mercy!

CHERUBINO (*stooping and peering*)   Am I mistaken? That hat I see with feathers outlined against the sky looks to me like Suzy.

COUNTESS   Oh, if the Count were to appear! (*The* COUNT *enters from the back*)

CHERUBINO (*goes up to* COUNTESS *and takes her hand, she pulls away*)   I'm right, it's that adorable girl named Sue! How could I mistake this soft hand, or that slight trembling . . . or the beating of my own heart! (*He tries to put the* COUNTESS's *hand against his heart*)

COUNTESS (*whispering*)   Go away!

CHERUBINO   Could it be that you took pity on my lot and came here where I have been hiding since afternoon?

COUNTESS   Figaro is coming.

COUNT (*stepping forward, aside*)   Isn't that Suzanne I see?

CHERUBINO (*to* COUNTESS)   I'm not afraid of Figaro and it's not him you're waiting for.

COUNTESS   Who then?

COUNT (*aside*)   Somebody is with her.

CHERUBINO   It's my lord, hussy, who asked you out here this morning when I hid behind the chair.

COUNT (*aside, furious*)   It's that infernal page again!

FIGARO (*aside*)   And they say it isn't nice to eavesdrop!

SUZANNE (*aside*)   The little chatterbox!

COUNTESS (*to* CHERUBINO)   Do me the kindness to go away.

CHERUBINO   Not without a reward for my compliance.

COUNTESS (*frightened*)   You claim—?

CHERUBINO (*with heat*)   Twenty kisses on your account first; then a hundred for your fair mistress.

COUNTESS   You would not dare!

CHERUBINO   Yes, I would! You're taking her place with my lord, I take his with you. The one who gets left is Figaro.

FIGARO (*aside*)   The rapscallion!

SUZANNE (*aside*)   Brash as a little page! (CHERUBINO *tries to kiss the* COUNTESS; *the* COUNT *comes between them and receives the kiss*)

COUNTESS (*retreating*)   Dear God!

FIGARO (*aside, hearing the sound of the kiss*)   It's a pretty baggage I'm marrying! (*Listens intently*)

CHERUBINO (feeling the COUNT'*s clothes; aside*)   It's my lord! (*He flees into the pavilion where* FANCHETTE *and* MARCELINE *are hiding*)

FIGARO (*approaching*)   I'm going to—

COUNT (*thinking the page still there*)   Since you don't repeat the kiss . . . (*lashes out with his hand*)

FIGARO (*coming within range, gets the slap*)   Ow!

COUNT   That's one paid off, anyhow.

FIGARO (*retreating and rubbing his cheek*)   This eavesdropping business isn't all pure gain.

SUZANNE (*laughing*)   Hahahaha!

COUNT (*to* COUNTESS *whom he mistakes for* SUZANNE)   That page is beyond belief—he gets slapped full in the face and goes off laughing.

FIGARO (*aside*)   He should be grieving for me!

COUNT   And he's intolerable: I can't take a step—But let's forget the puzzle or it will spoil the delight I feel in finding you here.

COUNTESS (*imitating* SUZANNE'*s voice*) Were you expecting me?

COUNT   What do you think, after your clever note? (*He takes her hand*) You're trembling.

COUNTESS I've been frightened.

COUNT   It wasn't to deprive you of a kiss that I took his. (*Kisses her on the forehead*)

COUNTESS Such liberties!

FIGARO (*aside*) The trollop!

SUZANNE (*aside*) The darling!

COUNT (*takes* COUNTESS's *hand*) How fine and soft your skin is! Your hand is more lovely than the Countess's.

COUNTESS (*aside*) What preconception will do!

COUNT   And this little arm, how firm and round . . . these pretty fingers full of grace and mischief!

COUNTESS (*speaking like* SUZANNE) And what of love . . . ?

COUNT   Love . . . is the fiction of the heart. Its history is pleasure, and hence you find me at your feet.

COUNTESS You do not love her any more?

COUNT   I love her very much, but three years make marriage so respectable.

COUNTESS What did you want from her?

COUNT (*caressing her*) What I find in you, my sweet.

COUNTESS But tell me what . . .

COUNT   I don't know . . . Less sameness, perhaps; more spice in your manner—something, I don't know what, which makes for charm; it's because you deny me sometimes, I don't know. Our wives think they can't do better than to love us. They take this for granted and love us and love us—if they love us—and they are so compliant and constant, always and without stint, that suddenly one day one finds satiety where one looked for happiness.

COUNTESS (*aside*) What a lesson to me!

COUNT To tell the truth, Suzy, I have often thought that when we seek elsewhere the pleasure we miss in them, it is because they make no effort to sustain our interest, to renew their attractions in love, to resurrect—so to speak—the delight of possession by affording that of variety.

COUNTESS (*vexed*) And so theirs is the whole responsibility?

COUNT (*laughing*) And the man has none, you mean? Well, can we change nature? Our task is to obtain . . .

COUNTESS Yes, and theirs—?

COUNT Is to . . . retain . . . That's generally overlooked.

COUNTESS Not by me.

COUNT Nor me.

FIGARO (*aside*) Nor me.

SUZANNE (*aside*) Nor me.

COUNT (*taking* COUNTESS'*s hand again*) There's an echo hereabouts; let's lower our voices. You for one needn't worry about holding a man! Love has fashioned you so fair and sprightly. Add a touch of caprice and you would be the most titillating mistress. (*Kisses her forehead*) My Suzy, a Castilian has nothing but his word of honor. I give you the ransom I promised, to redeem that old claim I no longer have upon the sweet concession you are about to make me.

COUNTESS (*curtsying*) Your Suzanne accepts everything.

FIGARO (*aside*) They don't exist more wanton than that.

SUZANNE (*aside*) It means good money in our pockets.

COUNT (*aside*) She's mercenary—all the better!

COUNTESS (*turning toward the back*) I see torches.

COUNT That's for your wedding. Let's go into the pavilion until they're by.

COUNTESS Without a light?

COUNT (*pulling her gently*) Why a light! We don't intend to read.

FIGARO (*aside*) She's going in, the drab! I thought so. (*He steps forward*)

COUNT (*turning around, in a voice of command*) Who's wandering around, there?

FIGARO (*angry*) Nobody's wandering; I'm coming on purpose!

COUNT (*to* COUNTESS) It's Figaro. (*He runs away*)

COUNTESS I'll follow you. (*She enters the pavilion on the right while the* COUNT *hides in the wood at the back*)

FIGARO (*trying to find them both*) I don't hear anything. They must have gone in. So here we are. (*In a changed voice*) Oh, you clumsy husbands who hire spies and toy with suspicion for months without confirming it, why not take your cue from me? I shadow my wife from the beginning, the first day. I listen secretly, and in a twinkling I know everything: it's enchanting—no doubts left, all is known. (*Pacing briskly*) Lucky that it doesn't bother me and that I'm no longer upset by her treachery. I've got them at last.

SUZANNE (*creeping up behind him; aside*) You're going to pay for those fine suspicions! (*Imitating the* COUNTESS) Who goes there?

FIGARO (*wildly*) "Who goes there?" A man who thinks the plague should have taken—

SUZANNE Why, it's Figaro!

FIGARO (*quickly*) My lady Countess!

SUZANNE Speak low!

FIGARO (*quickly*) Ah madam, how fortunate that you should have come. Where do you think my lord may be?

SUZANNE What does an ungrateful husband matter to me? Tell me rather—

FIGARO (*speaking still more rapidly*) And Suzanne, my bride, where do you imagine she might be?

SUZANNE *Please* lower your voice!

FIGARO Suzanne, my Suzy whom everybody thought so virtuous, who acted so modest! Well, they're locked up in there. I'm going to call out.

SUZANNE (*putting her hand on his mouth and forgetting to disguise her voice*) Don't call out!

FIGARO (*aside*) This is Suzy! God damn!

SUZANNE (*imitating the* COUNTESS) You seem upset.

FIGARO (*aside*) The minx! Trying to catch me!

SUZANNE We must avenge ourselves, Figaro.

FIGARO Do you feel a pressing need of it?

SUZANNE Am I not a woman? Men, though, have better means.

FIGARO (*confiding*) Madam, your presence is as necessary as mine. And women's means . . . are the best.

SUZANNE (*aside*) I'd like to slap the lout!

FIGARO (*aside*) Wouldn't it be fun if even before we're married . . .

SUZANNE But what kind of revenge is it that lacks the spice of love?

FIGARO If you see no signs of love, you may be sure I am only restrained by deference.

SUZANNE (*nettled*) I can't tell whether you mean that honestly, but you certainly don't say it gracefully.

FIGARO (*with comical fervor, kneeling*) Oh, madam, I worship you. But consider the time, the place, the circumstance, and let your anger supply the fire which my entreaty lacks.

SUZANNE (*aside*) My hand is itching.

FIGARO (*aside*) My heart is beating.

SUZANNE But, sir, have you reflected?

FIGARO Oh, yes, madam, yes indeed, I have reflected.

SUZANNE In anger and in love—

FIGARO Delay is fatal, I know. Your hand, madam.

SUZANNE (*in her own voice and slapping him*) Here it is.

FIGARO Lucifer, what a fist!

SUZANNE What fist?—is this the one? (*Slaps him again*)

FIGARO Now, what the devil? Are you playing windmill?

SUZANNE (*slapping him with each phrase*) "Ah, Lucifer, Suzanne!" Take *that* for your suspicion, and *that* for your revenge, and *that* for your schemes, and your insults, and your double dealing. Then you can say as you did this morning: "That's love for you!"

FIGARO (*laughing as he gets up*) By all the saints, it is!—pure love! What happiness, what bliss! Thrice-blessed Figaro! Hit me, belovèd, again and again. Only, when you're through painting me black and blue, Suzy, look kindly upon the luckiest man ever beaten by a woman.

SUZANNE The luckiest, you scoundrel? As if you weren't busy seducing the Countess with your pretty turns of phrase, to the point where I was forgetting myself and yielding in her place!

FIGARO As if I had mistaken the sound of your lovely voice!

SUZANNE (*laughing*) You recognized me, did you? I'll take my toll for that too.

FIGARO Just like a woman to beat a body and bear a grudge besides. But tell me by what good fortune I find you here when I thought you there. And these clothes, which fooled me at first, and now prove you innocent . . .

SUZANNE *You* are the innocent, to walk into a trap laid for someone else. Is it our fault if in trying to catch a fox we catch two?

FIGARO Who's catching the other?

SUZANNE His wife.

FIGARO His wife?

SUZANNE His wife.

FIGARO (*wildly*) Ah Figaro, go hang yourself on the nearest tree. You never guessed! His wife! Oh clever, clever, clever women. So all those resounding kisses . . .

SUZANNE Fell on my lady.

FIGARO And the one from the page?

SUZANNE On my lord.

FIGARO And this morning, behind the chair?

SUZANNE On nobody.

FIGARO Are you sure?

SUZANNE (*laughing*) Figaro! You know how fists fly about at dusk!

FIGARO (*seizes her hand and kisses it*) Yours are jewels to me. But the Count's in my face was fair enough.

SUZANNE Come, proud one, abase yourself.

FIGARO (*acting as he speaks*) Fair enough: on my knees, bowed low, prone and flat on the ground.

SUZANNE (*laughing*) The poor Count! What trouble he's gone to . . .

FIGARO (*rising and kneeling*) . . . to seduce his wife.

COUNT (*entering from the back and going straight to the pavilion on the right; aside*) I can't find her in the wood; perhaps she's stepped in here.

SUZANNE (*whispering to* FIGARO) There he goes.

COUNT (*at the open door of the pavilion*) Suzanne, are you there?

FIGARO (*low*) He's looking for her. I thought . . .

SUZANNE (*low*) He never recognized her.

FIGARO Let's finish him off, shall we? (*Kisses her hand noisily*)

COUNT (*turning round*) A man kneeling before the Countess . . . And I'm unarmed. (*He comes forward*)

FIGARO (*rising and disguising his voice*) Forgive me, madam, if I did not realize that this meeting place would be in the path of the festivities.

COUNT (*aside*) That's the man of this morning in the dressing room. (*He strikes his forehead*)

FIGARO But such a silly interference shan't postpone our pleasure.

COUNT (*aside*) Death and damnation!

FIGARO (*leading* SUZANNE *to the pavilion; aside*) He's cursing.

(*Aloud*) Let us hasten, madam, and repair the misfortune we suffered earlier when I jumped out of the window.

COUNT (*aside*)   Now I see it all!

SUZANNE (*near the pavilion on the left*)   Before we go in, make sure nobody is following. (*He kisses her forehead*)

COUNT (*shouting*)   Revenge! (SUZANNE *flees into the pavilion where* MARCELINE, FANCHETTE, *and* CHERUBINO *already are. The* COUNT *seizes* FIGARO *by the arm*)

FIGARO (*pretending great fright*)   It's the master!

COUNT   Ah, villain, it's you! Ho, somebody, come at once!
(*Enter* PETER, *booted and spurred*).

PETER   So there you are, my lord, at last.

COUNT   Good! Are you alone, Peter?

PETER   Back from Seville, hell for leather.

COUNT   Come close to me and shout very loud.

PETER (*at the top of his lungs*)   No more page in Seville than on the back of my hand—and that's a fact!

COUNT (*pushing him away*)   Stupid oaf!

PETER   Your lordship said I must shout aloud.

COUNT (*holding* FIGARO)   It was to call for help. Ho, there, somebody! Whoever hears me, come quick!

PETER   Figaro's here with me: what are you afraid of?

Enter BRIDLEGOOSE, BARTHOLO, BASIL, ANTONIO, *and* SUN-STRUCK, *followed by the wedding party carrying torches*).

BARTHOLO (*to* FIGARO)   You see: we came as soon as we heard you.

COUNT (*pointing to the pavilion on the left*)   Peter, guard that door. (PETER *goes*)

BASIL (*low to* FIGARO)   You caught him with Suzanne?

COUNT (*pointing to* FIGARO)   You, vassals, surround this man and answer for him with your lives.

BASIL   Oh, oh!

COUNT (*angry*) Be quiet. (*To* FIGARO, *freezingly*) Sir Knight, will you answer a few questions?

FIGARO (*coolly*) Who indeed could give me leave not to? You have command of everybody here except yourself.

COUNT (*mastering his fury*) Except myself?

ANTONIO That's the way to talk!

COUNT (*giving way to his anger*) If anything could make me angrier, it's the air of calmness he puts on.

FIGARO Are we like soldiers, killing and being killed for reasons they know nothing of? For my part, I always like to know what I'm angry about.

COUNT (*beside himself*) Murder! (*controlling himself*) Man of gentle birth who pretend not to know my reasons, would you at least do us the favor of telling us what lady you have brought into this pavilion?

FIGARO (*mischievously pointing to the other*) Into that one?

COUNT (*quickly*) Into this.

FIGARO (*coldly*) That's different. It's a young lady who honors me with her favors.

BASIL (*surprised*) Oh?

COUNT (*quickly*) You heard him, gentlemen?

BARTHOLO (*surprised*) We heard him.

COUNT And this young person is otherwise unattached?

FIGARO (*coldly*) I know that a great lord paid her some attentions for a while. But whether it be that he neglected her or that she likes me better, I am the one preferred.

COUNT (*quickly*) The one pref- (*restraining himself*) At least he is candid. What he has just admitted, I myself have seen and heard, gentlemen, from the mouth of his accomplice. I give you my word on it.

BRIDLEGOOSE (*petrified*) His ac-complice!

COUNT (*in fury*) Now, when dishonor is public, so must be the revenge! (*He goes into the pavilion*)

ANTONIO He's right.

BRIDLEGOOSE (*to* FIGARO) Who took who-o-o's wife?

FIGARO (*laughing*) No one had that special satisfaction.

COUNT (*speaking from inside the pavilion and tugging at some-one not yet identifiable*) It is no use, madam, the hour has struck and you are doomed. (*He comes out and turns to the rest without looking*) How fortunate that there lives no pledge of our hateful union—!

FIGARO (*calling out*) Cherubino!

COUNT The page!

BASIL Haha!

COUNT Always the damned page! What were you doing in that room?

CHERUBINO (*shyly*) I was hiding, as you ordered me to do.

PETER What use was it to nearly kill a horse!

COUNT Go in there, Antonio, and bring before her judge the criminal who has dishonored me.

BRIDLEGOOSE Is it my lady that you are l-looking for?

ANTONIO 'Tis Providence, by gum, for your carryings-on all over the countryside.

COUNT (*furious*) Get in there! (ANTONIO *goes in*)

COUNT You shall see, gentlemen, that the page was not alone.

CHERUBINO (*shyly*) It would have been hard on me if a gentle soul had not sweetened the bitter pill.

ANTONIO (*pulling out someone not recognizable at first*) Come, my lady, don't make me coax you, everybody knows you went in.

FIGARO (*calling out*) My little cousin!

BASIL Haha!

COUNT Fanchette!

ANTONIO (*turns around*) By jiminy 'twas right smart, my lord, to pick on me to show the company it's my daughter caused all the randan, now wasn't it?

COUNT (*indignant*) Who could suppose she was in there? (*He tries to go in*)

BARTHOLO (*interposing*) Allow me, my lord. All this is far too upsetting for you; but perhaps I can deal with it in cold blood. (*He goes in*).

BRIDLEGOOSE It's certainly too confusing for me.

BARTHOLO (*speaking from inside and coming out*) Do not be afraid, madam, no one will hurt you, I promise you. (*He turns around and cries out*) Marceline!

BASIL Haha!

FIGARO (*laughing*) A madhouse! My mother in it too!

ANTONIO The jades are playing who can be the worst.

COUNT (*outraged*) What is that to me? It's the Countess . . . (SUZANNE *comes out, her face behind a fan*) Ah, there she is at last, gentlemen. (*He takes her violently by the arm*) What does such an odious woman deserve, gentlemen—?

(SUZANNE *falls on her knees, bowing her head*).

COUNT Never, never! (FIGARO *kneels next to her*)

COUNT (*louder*) Never! (MARCELINE *kneels beside the others*)

COUNT (*still louder*) Never, never! (*They all kneel*)

COUNT (*beside himself*) Never, not if there were a hundred of you!

COUNTESS (*coming out of the other pavilion*) At least, I can make one more.

COUNT (*looking alternately at* SUZANNE *and the* COUNTESS) What do I see?

BRIDLEGOOSE (*laughing*) What d'you kn-n-know, it's my lady!

COUNT (*trying to lift her up*) It was you, Countess? (*In a supplicating tone*) Only the most generous forgiveness . . .

COUNTESS (*laughing*) In my place, you would say "Never, never!" whereas I, for the third time today, forgive you unconditionally. (*She gets up*)

SUZANNE (*getting up*) And so do I.

MARCELINE (*getting up*) And I.

FIGARO (*getting up*) And I. There's an echo hereabouts. (*All get up*).

COUNT An echo! I tried to outsmart them and they fooled me like a child.

COUNTESS (*laughing*) Don't act as if you were sorry, my lord.

FIGARO (*brushing off his knees with his hat*) A day like today is ideal training for an ambassador.

COUNT (*to* SUZANNE) That note sealed with a pin? . . .

SUZANNE Madam dictated it.

COUNT The answer is overdue. (*He kisses the* COUNTESS's *hand*)

COUNTESS Each will regain his own. (*She gives the purse to* FIGARO *and the diamond to* SUZANNE)

SUZANNE (*to* FIGARO) Still another dowry!

FIGARO (*striking the purse*) That makes three. But this one took some contriving.

SUZANNE Like our marriage.

SUNSTRUCK What about the bride's garter? Can I have it?

COUNTESS (*taking out the ribbon from her bosom*) The garter? It was in her clothes. Here you are. (*She throws the ribbon; the boys try to scramble for it*)

CHERUBINO (*swiftly picking it up*) Try and get it!

COUNT (*laughing*) Since you're so touchy a gentleman, what made you laugh so hard when I boxed your ear?

CHERUBINO (*taking a step backward and half drawing his sword*) My ear, colonel?

FIGARO (*comically angry*) He got it on *my* cheek, as always happens when lords mete out justice.

COUNT (*laughing*) On your cheek, ha, ha, ha, isn't that good, what do you say, dear Countess?

COUNTESS (*abstracted and returning to reality*) Indeed, dear Count, I do—for life, unswervingly, I swear it.

COUNT (*slapping* BRIDLEGOOSE *on the shoulder*)   And you, Bridle-goose, let us have your opinion.

BRIDLEGOOSE   On what has taken p-place, my lord? Well, my opinion is that I d-don't know what to think, and that's my opinion.

ALL (*together*)   A very sound judgment!

FIGARO   I was poor and despised. When I showed a little clever-ness, hatred dogged me. Now with a pretty girl and some money . . .

BARTHOLO (*laughing*)   Everybody will crowd around you!

FIGARO   Do you think so?

BARTHOLO   I know my kind.

FIGARO (*bowing to the spectators*)   Aside from my wife and my goods, you are welcome to all I have. (*The orchestra plays the introduction to the entertainment*)

BASIL

Triple dowry, handsome wife—
To a husband, what largesse!
'Gainst a lord or beardless page
Only fools feel jealous rage.
Let the Latin proverb bless
Man's incalculable life:

FIGARO   Don't I know that proverb! (*sings*) "Happy those of noble birth!"

BASIL   No you *don't* know it! (*sings*) "Happy those who own the earth!"

SUZANNE

Let a man his wife betray
He is boastful, all are gay;

Let his wife indulge her whim
She is punished, unlike him.
If you ask why this is so,
'Tis the stronger's wicked law.

MARCELINE

Every man his mother knows,
Her who'd give her life for him.
But beyond this all is dim—
How explain love's secret lure?
FIGARO (*breaking in*) Secret, though the end disclose
That the offspring of a boor
May turn out a gentleman.

FIGARO

By the accident of birth,
One is shepherd, t'other king.
Chance made lord and underling,
Only genius threads the maze:
Twenty kings are fed on praise
Who in death are common earth,
While Voltaire immortal stays.

CHERUBINO

Flighty sex we all adore,
You who torment all our days,
Everyone complains of you;
In the end we kneel and sue.
To the pit thus players do:
Such a one professes scorn
Who would crawl to earn your bays.

FIGARO

Jack McJohn, the jealous lout,
Hoped to have both wife and peace;
Hired a dog to roam about
In the garden, fierce and free;
Barks as claimed in guaranty;
All are bitten by the beast,
Save the lover from whom leased.

COUNTESS

There's a wife who's proudly prude
Though she loves her husband not;
There's another, nearly lewd,
Swears she loveth none but he;
Now the worthiest is she,
Never swearing this or that,
Who but strives for honesty.

COUNT

Any woman far from Court
Who believes in duty strict
In romance falls somewhat short.
I prefer the derelict:
Like a piece of currency,
Stamped with one man's effigy,
She can serve the needs of all.

SUZANNE

If there should a moral lurk
In this mad yet cheerful work,
For the sake of gaiety,
Pray accept it as a whole.

Thus does Nature, sensibly,
Using pleasures we pursue,
Lead up gently to her goal.

BRIDLEGOOSE

Now dear sirs, the c-comic art,
Which you shortly mean to j-judge,
Apes the l-life of all of you
Sitting there and taking p-part.
When annoyed you bear a g-grudge
But although you grumble l-long,
All our d-doings end in song.